THE ART & SIGNS OF SPIRITUAL AWAKENING

The Art & Signs of Spiritual Awakening

The 21 Signs - It's Your Time

LESLIE A. PARAMORE

Heart Centered Productions

I wish to dedicate this book to over 7.9 billion souls who are currently a part of our grand awakening. I affectionally acknowledge our Creator, spiritual guides, angels, ascended masters, and any portion of goodness and love that exists. Without all of you, the unfolding of this book would not have been possible.

My heart also expresses deep gratitude to the man who would get me the moon if I asked him. My husband, playmate, friend, and confident, Scott Paramore.

To my mom and dad, the two souls that carried me into the world. I thank you for creating a foundation that was built with empathy, compassion, caring, respect, and love.

Finally, to my four children, Jessica, Curtis, Corey and Corin; my greatest teachers in life.

Contents

Preface

Congratulations on choosing to participate in this unique material highlighting the signs of spiritual awakening & ascension. The information provided here is presented in a way that will be easy for you to understand and integrate into your personal life. There is a common buzz word among the spiritual community that presents itself in the form of a question, "Are you awake?" To the average human, it may sound like a foolish question to ask someone when it is obvious that the person is completely awake, standing directly in front of you, with eyes wide open. Yet, I now present to you the same question. "Are you awake?" Most of us who have been experiencing the signs of awakening will understand that question, because as we become more awake spiritually, we realize just how deeply asleep we were! At least that was the case with me.

A spiritual awakening is simply a newfound perception or experience of life that comes on rapidly or gradually. Every soul will experience their personal awakening differently, yet many of the symptoms or signs of awakening are the same. I suppose you could compare it to how you feel when you first wake up in the morning. You are a little groggy, and maybe a little disoriented, as you wipe the sleepy film away from your eyes to clear your vision for the day. Sometimes it takes a bit of effort to wake up, but the inventible happenstance will eventually come, for everyone.

There are many who are experiencing symptoms that can at times feel confusing and uncomfortable and it is for this reason I felt inspired to offer a course that can help support you through this beautiful metamorphosis that you are currently experiencing. At this time, you may feel like a caterpillar crawling through life, wondering what you are going to climb over next, however, something within you is calling you to ascend higher into other ways of thinking and being. To do so, you must first venture into unfamiliar territory just as a real caterpillar climbs a tree, fastening itself onto the perfect branch of transformation. I would ask that you let this course be that branch of security and transformation for you as we move you through the life changing experiences that are showing up for you right now. As you break through the layers of the cocoon you have been sleeping in, you will find that you were never meant to be limited in life. I suppose you could compare the cocoon to your physical body that acts as a temporally veil of forgetfulness; the thing that has kept you in a deep slumber. As you become more spiritually aware of your real identity, the veil of your body will become lighter, freer, and more alive than ever! You were never meant to crawl. Every experience that you have been through has brought you to this experience. Just like the butterfly, you will break free of your cocoon of limitation and fly to your greatest spiritual potential presented right before you.

Your spiritual awakening will bring you to new horizons of possibility within your life. You will become more expansive, and your life will transform to new ways of thinking, being and believing. In fact, your once believing state anchored in the limitation of your cocoon, will transform to an inner knowing that is virtually impossible to describe through words, unless you have experienced it for yourself. Are you ready to break free? Let's get started!

Introduction

We are living in uncertain times where individuals just like you are going through life challenging shifts toward spiritual evolution. It is a revolution that very few can ignore as life moves each of us into an evolved state of consciousness. With so much uncertainty and upheaval directly on the horizon, people are learning new ways to navigate their way through these paradigm shifts.

It can feel unsettling as the earth vibrationally shifts beneath our feet. It is for this reason we have created this groundbreaking book, "The Art & Signs of Spiritual Awakening," which is specifically designed to support you through the planetary shifts now occurring. Although these subtle and sometimes abrupt changes may feel disorienting, leaving individuals feeling displaced, let me reassure you that the birthing pains of ascension are lifting us to greater possibilities as individuals and as a collective species.

As you move through this material we will delve deep together as we offer newly channeled information about the journey of your soul and its timely process of awakening to ascension. We will discuss topics like spiritual DNA vs physical DNA and what roles they play in the ascension process. We will explore your personal energy patterns and their connections to the internal and external world. We will uncover how divine communication works with your body and your soul, and many more pieces of essential information designed to offer you the tools necessary for your awareness. The information presented will no doubt challenge you to think outside of the common conditioning of mankind and into the heights of spiritual knowing and mastery.

Throughout this material, we will also outline 21 indicators or symptoms of spiritual awakening that you may find yourself identifying with on multiple levels. You'll receive the much-awaited answers for the deep purposes of these indicators that are now showing up in your life. Along with these indicators we will also share pertinent and applicable suggestions and exercises that will support you in navigating your way through these life altering changes.

Let's face it change isn't always easy, especially as we are awakening to the unknown parts of ourselves. As a spiritual channeler and healer, I have great empathy and compassion for those who have come to me, lost in questions pertaining to these sudden life changes they are faced with. Perhaps you can identify with these feelings as well. Perhaps your life could use some clarity and direction right now as you are led to remember the truth already within you. It is truly an honor to join you on this soul journey. As we navigate our way through this book together, you'll discover that our connection was no accident as truth reveals itself from within.

Chapter 1

The Earthquake in My House

I feel it's important to share the profound shift that literally shook me into my own spiritual awakening. It should be noted that I was raised with no belief systems instilled regarding any type of Creator, God, Supreme Deity, or any concepts of Universal Consciousness. I was, however, taught many beautiful concepts about love, kindness, compassion, being mindful of others, working hard, and being the best that I could be as a meaningful contributor to this planet. I was painfully shy, socially awkward, and timid. I wasn't what I would call a well-adjusted child. I simply felt out of place; like I somehow didn't belong in this somewhat peculiar place called, earth. The principles I was taught as a child set a foundation for my life, however, it was up to me to build the rest of my house. Nothing could prepare the innocence of my childhood to enter into the rude awakenings that took place in my early years of adulthood, as I tried to make sense of my world.

My early adult years came and looking back now, I realize that I was deeply wrapped in a cocoon of forgetfulness and didn't even know it. The thick walls of my cocoon seemed to squeeze every aspect of my heart into the dark night of the soul. Total forgetfulness buried me as I experienced three painful marriages while desperately trying to find my way back to my disoriented self. I understand now that ultimately the marriages were a gift to my awakening self, and I have nothing but gratitude for the lessons learned during those times of my life. The marriages showed me everything conceivable that I was not, as they served me on so many levels of my awakening. Those emotional holes within me desperately grasped at anything that might show me love, that might show me acceptance, that might show me that I was worthy of something, anything. I needed a sense of belonging in a world that felt so foreign, yet it was I who abandoned myself. I had surely lost my true identity by looking outward to the external things of the world. The dark night was surely upon me, as I was blind to the light within me.

My early life was filled with painful lessons which seemed to be constantly shouting at me to wake up from the dream I was in. In search for meaning, truth, purpose, and my divine path, I had been engaged in studying various religions throughout my life. Although these religions served me on many levels and in many capacities, I came to a space where I was seeking more answers than what I was receiving. It was only then at that pinnacle moment, when I stood at the head of many paths that I was led to the one true path of my divine heart. I knew intuitively that my heart was calling me to new levels of spiritual consciousness and awakening. It was a familiar voice that I could not ignore. It was at that decisive moment that I was determined to take the sacred journey into myself. I pushed against the walls of the cocoon I had been bound in and with great exerted effort I broke through. And with that victory I found beautiful transformative things like forgiveness, compassion, empathy, and the love that I am. Like all butterflies emerging from their cocoons, I had to leave the cocoon behind. All the pain, disappointment, shame, regret, and the disillusioned parts of myself withered away with the cocoon, as I took flight into my new journey of awakening.

Through many years of searching for deeper meaning, greater purpose, and conscious connections, I found myself being drawn to healing work. I became a massage therapist, and expanded my gifts into energy healing, while using several other accommodating tools to support many in their awakening process.

As an intuitive channeler and healer, I began to be more conscious of my path and the direction I felt called to be on. I began to strengthen my body through proper eating, exercising, and getting plenty of rest upon direct spiritual guidance from the universal consciousness that we are all a part of. I was specifically guided to strengthen my body and to prepare to work with the new energy that would be channeled through me. Everything appeared to be going smoothly in my life as I became more confident as a healer and made the adjustments and natural changes to support my spiritual growth and awakening.

Just when I seemed to be finally settling into my life, I was awoken in the early hours of the morning with excruciating pain shooting through my solar plexus chakra and then up through my chest. It was a wakeup call I truly wasn't prepared for. I sat up abruptly, slightly panicked, with shock coursing through my emotional body. My heart was pounding uncontrollably against my chest wall. I knew something unusually terrifying was occurring in that abrupt moment and it appeared that despite my healing gifts, there was nothing I could do about it. The pain was instantaneous and subsided after just a few short seconds, yet without warning or any divine explanation, my physical body began to shake uncontrollably. My electrical circuits were crashing.

In my shocked state, I made a rushed visit to the emergency room, hoping to get relief from the shaking and some much-needed answers. It was obvious to the medical team that I was in distress. I went through a series of extensive medical tests, bloodwork, a Cat Scan, an EKG, and every test imaginable. The doctors spent several hours at the computer reviewing possible causes for such a unique medical crisis. They were left empty handed and deeply perplexed.

As the doctors entered the room where I waited with anticipation, I continued to shake outwardly, and inwardly I was terrified to hear the results. The doctor remarked that my body was in pristine condition, and he joked that I was built like a racehorse and that the only thing that was out of the norm was that my dopamine levels, which are the feel-good hormones, were off the charts. We all had a relieved laugh as the nurse on duty commented that she wished she could have experienced high levels of dopamine. The doctors could offer me nothing more than some empathy and compassion along with some sedatives that I refused to take. The phenomenon of the shaking could not be explained, and I was left with no where to look but inward for the answers.

My shaking episodes interrupted my days with relentless consistency, taking a period of several months to process. Working with the new energy was extremely difficult and challenging for my mind, body, and spirit. It seemed like my body had to relearn how to feel calm inside. I had to learn how to turn a dimmer switch down on a light, filled with a high frequency energy. My wakeup call involved my body shaking for eight long months.

Although I did not understand this experience at the time of its occurrence, I now attribute this experience to the fact that much of what I was doing in my life's healing work through energy channeling got overloaded. In short, my circuits got overloaded and for lack of a better phrase, I blew a fuse. Imagine plugging your toaster into a high voltage outlet, that's meant to run your stove. I'm surprised there wasn't smoke coming out of my ears.

In my human exuberance to serve others in this capacity, I unknowingly activated way too many circuits in my body. I suppose the experience could be compared to overeating, where one is left with a huge stomachache to deal with, but only in this case, this was spiritual energy that my body was trying desperately to digest.

Learning to digest this new energy took a considerable amount of discipline on my part. Much of this was accomplished through meditation, powerful affirmations, exercise and sleeping when I could. Several months after, the powerful energy finally settled to a simple low humming vibrational frequency within my body, which I now experience as the loving and healing vibration of the divine within.

The earthquake within the walls of my physical house was finally over, however, like any aftermath after a disaster, there was still repair and rebuilding to do. The emotional and mental vulnerabilities that were literally shaken loose showed themselves to me, face to face, heart to heart, soul to soul.

The day my house shook is one that forever changed my life. It was the wakeup call I needed to expand the relationship I now have with myself. It built a bridge of loving communication between my physical body and my spiritual body. This isn't to suggest that I am fully awakened. I am still learning to integrate the two parts of me as one. I continue to learn and grow through my own awakening process right along with you, as in the ultimate reality of the divine, we must bring forth this awakening of ascension together.

Chapter 2

Are You Awake?

Okay here you are probably wondering what is happening with your life. It may seem that nothing makes sense anymore as you awaken from the illusionary dream you have been in. You are now wiping the film from your physical eyes and beginning to open your third eye, which is also referred to as your intuitive eye or third eye. Perhaps as the sedative anesthesia of life wears off, things still look a little foggy and you may feel a little confused and displaced from your once familiar surroundings. Everything seems to be screaming at you to wake up! The screaming might manifest itself as unexpected physical symptoms within your body that no doctor can explain through testing, yet the symptoms are undeniably present with you. It would appear that despite negative test results that pain, or unusual physical sensations have taken up permanent housing within your body and you just cannot seem to shake it off no matter how much positive thinking you do. 101 positive affirmations failed, and you're about done with the superficial things of the world.

In your awakening process, that symbolic screaming might felt like an earthquake, where strong emotions erupt unexpectedly, disrupting the middle of your day, and in the most inconvenient times. Internally you may think you are losing it, but externally you don't dare show it because those around you seem to have their lives together, and let's face it, being vulnerable just isn't considered cool these days. With the demands of life and the demands on your time, maybe you need to keep it together too, for the sake of appearing sane even though you may feel otherwise.

The problem with repression is one can only deny it for so long. The truth eventually comes out. How long have you been denying yourself by sleeping away your life in the physical world? Right now, you may think that you are your physical body. You may think that you are your titles, your possessions, or your position in life, but that could not be further from the truth. You have learned over time, to just carry on like everyone else on the conveyor belt of life, clocking in and clocking out of your mind, time after time, after time. Everyone seems to be on auto pilot, going through the motions, yet not really getting anywhere. And now, here you are finally at a point in time where you can no longer keep it together for the sake of looking normal. Something within you is screaming at you to wake up. You are long past due. You have slept in way too long and the convey belt of your life is now broken. It is time to step off the artificial machinery of your mind and to open the portals of your heart now awakening.

Let me reassure you at this time that you are not losing your life or your mind. You are simply going through a beautiful metamorphosis, initiating the birthing of your true identity into your new reality. Your birthing is occurring at the perfect time; not one minute too soon or one minute too late. Just as the butterfly pushes against the walls of the cocoon to be set free, the inner essence of you, your infinite soul, is pushing against what you once thought you were. Trust in the light that is now coming. You are more ready than you know.

Chapter 3

The Process of Awakening

Before we delve into this material, I'd like to briefly cover how we are going to support you in your awakening process or the birth of the new you. One important thing to note about anyone's awakening process is that not all symptoms or what I refer to as birthing pains will show up at once. And not all symptoms indicate that there is something terribly wrong with your life. I use the word symptom because it is a word that most individuals can identify with. We can also use the word indicator or sign to reflect what we are wanting to convey here. An example of a symptom of awakening might be you begin having deeper spiritual insights which would be a positive indicator that you are awakening. Other symptoms can feel somewhat negative, like feeling unusually moody or agitated. So, in short, a symptom of waking up can feel either positive or negative and it can also be received or greeted either positively or negatively depending on pure choice of the individual.

As mentioned earlier, sometimes a symptom or indicator of awakening can come on rapidly, while another symptom or sign can come on gradually. The important thing to remember is the heart of your beautiful soul or higher self knows exactly what it is doing. It is now in the driver's seat of your life, being your personal birthing coach as you emerge from your cocoon.

Trust that you are supported in this process no matter what may show up as a symptom. As you move forward through this material, you will learn to breathe through uncertainty, and emerge feeling stronger and more confident on your expansive journey of awakening.

Another important piece to note is that not everyone experiences every awakening symptom in the same way. Some symptoms may feel more intense, like feelings of extreme anxiety, while others may be somewhat more manageable like limited sleep. In addition, some awakening signs may be so subtle that you will hardly notice them at all. Much of your personal experience will depend on how adaptable you are to change. If you resist the transformation, chances are you will have a much more difficult time processing what is occurring through your personal metamorphosis. Breathe and believe the best outcomes are being orchestrated for your highest realization in the light of your reality.

Some other things to consider before delving into this material is that certain awakening symptoms may show up in your life, and not necessarily in another person's life. For instance, in the material presented, we outline 21 awakening symptoms. Does this mean that you must master every single symptom to be considered spiritually awake? Fortunately for us, it doesn't work that way, because not everyone's life experiences are the same. Allow me to give you an example.

John may have experienced a childhood eating extremely healthy, being raised with a plentiful garden, that yields fresh fruits and vegetables and therefore has continued that natural pattern of eating into his adulthood. As a result, he probably won't experience any symptoms of awakening such as the urge to change his superb eating habits, whereas Jackie may have grown up eating fast food due to modern conveniences, and at some point, she may feel the urge to navigate toward healthier foods throughout her awakening process. So, you see, things like lifestyle, personal perceptions, belief systems, and also your unique experiences can often determine what symptoms may show up in your awakening process. No matter what it will be the perfect recipe to shake things up to wake things up.

And finally, another thing to make note of is that not all individuals are experiencing signs that indicate waking up. Some are still sleeping, completely caught up in the world and its many distractions. The mind has been deeply conditioned to think that we are here to have this physical experience – to be born, to live and to die, yet there is so much more to life than the life you've been living. All are awakening in their own timetable. As you awaken to new ways of thinking and being, you may be tempted to shout it from the rooftops, however, one cannot shake another into waking up no more than one can cause a butterfly to emerge from its cocoon before it's ready. All is in divine timing for every soul's awakening.

One last thing before we move on. I cannot express enough how grateful I am that you felt drawn to this material. Some unseen force somehow synchronically connected the energy to bring you to this place. It is a sure sign that you are waking up and I am so pleased to share this information with you. I too have gone through my own awakening which I confess was not always easy, yet looking back now, I can see the wisdom of every experience I was called to pass through. It is through these personal experiences, that I have been able to compile a list of awakening signs to share with you. When my spiritual awakening was happening, I really had no idea what was going on, yet I somehow intuitively knew that something was calling me to emerge from the darkness of the cocoon and into the light of a new day. Now, I cannot tell you how your awakening will be experienced by you, however, I can share what supported me through some exceedingly difficult times.

Just how awake are you? That question remains to be seen. You will be the observer as you move through the content of this material measuring yourself against the signs provided here. Let's move on, shall we?

"We have played many roles. Each of us brilliantly beautiful. We have had our seasons to turn the page, to write the words, to listen intently, to hold sacred space, and to share our heart when our spirit has been led to do so. We are writing our story together. Everyone is a portion of the ONE eternal love. Not one poor, but abundant. Not one lost, but found. Not one forgotten, but remembered. Not one tarnished, but infinitely valued."

-Leslie Paramore

Chapter 4

The Signs of Awakening

To support you in understanding the awakening symptoms or signs that may be occurring in your life, we will outline 21 predominant awareness's that most often occur for the average person during this process of internal transformation. Keep in mind that this does not mean that the 21 signs outlined in this material are all conclusive because I believe as we continue to wake up, we will be called to go through a much more refined process that moves us closer and closer to spiritual mastery and eventual spiritual ascension. Just as the butterfly has stages of development, from egg, to caterpillar, to cocoon, to butterfly, we too have stages of growth that we too must pass through.

Our birthright as spiritual beings are to awaken to the I Am presence of the God within. As we do so, we will experience a conscious shift in our being, mentally, emotionally, physically, and spiritually, filtering out any dense energy on every level, until we are so purified, we eventually obtain spiritual ascension through spiritual mastery. We could compare this process to what a metal worker does through the process of moving impurities out of metal. The metal is melted to such a severe degree that it purifies the gold, silver, or other types of precious metals. Once the metal is melted to the purified state, the dross or mass of solid impurities rises to the top of the boiled mixture and is removed before the precious metal cools. This is an accurate analogy of how our hearts are purified through life. With each awakening experience, the parts that no longer belong to us, rise like dross, and naturally fall away from our hearts. As you continue your journey, be prepared for things to fall away, like unhealthy relationships, old patterns or habits, old belief systems, stagnant jobs, or anything that no longer wishes to be a part of the expanded version of your new self. Does a butterfly carry its cocoon with it as it prepares for flight? No . . . it leaves it behind, just as you will leave things behind until you are light enough to fly!

As you move through exploring the material offered here, reframe how you look at these awakening experiences being reflected to you. Instead of seeing yourself as a wounded butterfly, emerging from the cocoon or dark night of the soul, you are now experiencing new divine opportunities for your heart to explore advanced expressions of light. Every time you push against the walls of the cocoon, you are allowing flecks of brilliant light to filter through you, offering greater visions as you explore new paths of spiritual perception.

A butterfly never questions its journey. It lets the sun dry its wings as it sits in stillness after breaking free from the limiting effects of its cocoon. You also can let the natural rays of the sun dry the tears you have often shed through your awakening and prepare for flight. You've made it this far, so don't worry about where you are going. The only place you can go from here is up.

Chapter 5

The Race to Ascension

When we are going through a spiritual awakening it can be helpful to know why. The whys can offer incentives and encouragement to keep going, to keep believing and to keep rising to the next marker of your awakening. Imagine a marathon runner who has trained tirelessly for the big race. The athlete begins at the starting line, eager to get going and then the moment of the experience begins. With great strength and eagerness, the athletic legs pound against the surface of the earth, and the heart pounds right along with them. The blood pulsates through the body like spiritual fuel, and the breath expands the lungs with what seems like the breath of God. Hours go by, yet the athlete continues to run, and the soul finds the strength to keep going despite the pain that is showing up in the physical body. The body pushes through the pain, determined to prove to itself that it can master every obstacle met on the course. The soul has the heart to win the race and the body is finely tuned for the ride of a lifetime. The momentum builds, the spirits are high, and the supernatural body is literally flying through time, distance, and space. It's magical and magnificent at the same time. Both body and spirit are working together like a finely tuned machine and the crowds cheer at such a sight. In time, the sun sets, the crowds go home, the night brings in a chill, and everyone goes to sleep. Yet the athlete still runs because the race was never about the applause from the crowds or the recognition of a trophy. The race continued because the athlete knew there would be a sense of accomplishment as the journey pushed through to the unknown depths of the heart.

Now imagine what would happen in that journey if there was no finish line in sight. Would the soul and body keep running together in unison? The answer is apparent. In the human condition, the eternal soul would continue to run, yet the dense physical body would wear out, unable to finish the race. The spirit is willing, but the flesh is weak. In order to ascend, the physical body and spiritual body must learn to work together. Their energies must resonate at the same vibration in order to win the race. They must ascend to greatness together, for in the final destination of ascension, one was never meant to be one without the other.

There are many thoughts about what ascension is. For the purpose of this information before you, we will simply share what has been shown through the spiritual channeling that has been received. Some viewing this material may understand the term spiritual ascension by other means, while others may be left with no real reference to turn to. No matter where you are in this moment in terms of beliefs or non-beliefs, keep in mind that we are all learning and growing together. We offer to you with the highest integrity of our soul to consider the ideas we present to the individual representation of you. You then can choose what resonates with your life's path and leave the rest behind. For the purposes of personal awareness and collective congruency, we will define the term spiritual ascension in relatively simple terms. *"Spiritual ascension begins with the direct coherence and communication between the physical body and the spiritual body, naturally and gradually merging the divine intelligences of both bodies. The spiritual body is symbolic, or a representation of the heavens and the physical body is symbolic or a representation of the earth. In the ascension process the two shall become one in every aspect."*

In discussing ascension, we have been taught in many traditional teachings that the heavenly realms are some far off place that is virtually unobtainable if we aren't living a certain Godly lifestyle. Depending on what we've been taught in our culture, there tends to be exact rules that dictate the pathway to the heavens paved with promises of gold. We weren't born with this knowledge; we were taught it by others as we collectively descended into the world, adopting these teachings into our belief systems. Consequently, we continue to experience the division between our minds and hearts, as we listen to external voices urging us to their truth, instead of the pure truth we once came here with. So, let's pretend that heaven really is a far-off place reserved for only the pure of heart. If this is true, wouldn't it make perfect sense that in order to get to this very far-off place, that we must first create and experience heaven within ourselves? How can we be divided internally and expect to get anywhere in life, let alone heaven? That path to the divine love of heaven begins within each of us.

Chapter 6

The Two Shall Become One

In terms of the process of ascension, we must first become one with ourselves, no longer being divided between the mind and the heart. The very division of such is what keeps us from ascending to the I Am presence of the God within. There are many names associated with this idea of oneness that humans have a natural and innate tendency to gravitate toward. Just as a child is chemically bonded to its mother, we are also spiritually attuned to bond with the infinite and eternal love within. Some may have heard this infinite force of one referenced by these names: Nirvana, Divine Love, Christ Consciousness, Saved, Sealed, Resurrected, Eternal Bliss, and Heaven, to name just a few. Although powerfully displayed and defended by different belief systems, they all point to the same thing, the complete and eventual ascension of a soul.

Imagine for a moment that your soul specifically came to this planet to learn to become master over the physical elements. One aspect of that physical element is your body to which you have been specifically assigned. It's your house and you are the keeper at the inn. As you have played the role of the keeper at the inn; the place where there was no room for divine love to give birth, or the Christ child within, your body may suddenly find itself in distress because of its separation from what we know as God or divine love. As a pre-life contract, we are proposing that it was your soul's divine mission and everyone else's divine mission to connect with their physical bodies and bring them back in one piece.

How are we doing with that? Not so good. In a world that is riddled with disease, disharmony, and delusions, we have a long way to go. In a world that is divided internally and externally, individually, and collectively, the marathon we are running together has no real end in sight. What are we running from and what are we running for if not to ascend together? We cannot cross the bridge to ascension until we bridge the gap between our minds and our hearts, individually and collectively.

The material here will challenge your current belief systems. It will birth you into new ways of thinking and being. At the same time, it will support your personal awakening process as you learn to bridge the gap between your own mind and heart. As the awakening within you is given permission to expand through the experiences laid out in this material, your mind and your heart will learn to become connected as one, just as the body and soul were intended to be connected as one. It is then that your personal awakening and movement toward spiritual ascension can truly begin. From biblical reference we share the following words for your consideration:

"I say, 'You are gods; you are all children of the Most High."
Psalms 82:6

"Don't you realize that all of you together are the temple of God and that the Spirit of God lives in you?"
1st Corinthians 3:16

Chapter 7

The House of Your Soul

Let's continue on to the next awareness as we awaken to the truths you already know within. As mentioned earlier, we have all been spiritually commissioned to become masters over our physical bodies and then to also learn how to master our physical experiences in life. Nothing is happenstance. Nothing is coincidental. Nothing is synchronistic. Everything is by divine design including the physical body you are currently housed in. Do you like what you are living in?

What does your house or body look like on the inside and on the outside? What does it feel like to live in your physical body? If you could compare your body to a house that you've taken up residency in, would your house be up to date, well-kept and orderly, or a maze of cluttered obstacles and barricades that you've got to find your way through? Does your body feel light or heavy? Is it soft or hard? Is it flexible or stiff? Is it energized or tired? Is the space you are housed in appreciating in value or depreciating? Who is charge of your house and its upkeep, physically, emotionally, mentally, and spiritually?

Let's take this a step further, if you purchased a rundown shack that needed some extra care and maintenance to make it livable, would you be content to live in that shack that was falling apart, or would you invest your time and energy in creating a better place to live? The question is, why do we spend so much time fixing our cars and upgrading our homes, yet we have been consistently known to neglect our own bodies, the very thing that is essential for the expression of our souls? I think you can see where we now have some upgrades and maintenance to do.

Our bodies are intelligent, and they have ways of communicating to us when things are out of alignment or out of balance. When our bodies are not functioning at their optimal levels, we experience pain, chills, fevers, stiffness, weakness, fatigue and in a worst-case scenario, our bodies die. Consider this for a moment: your soul holds a distinct vibration that was predesigned to merge with your physical body. Think of your soul as a master key that opens the portals of your physical body. It enters in as the keeper of the inn. As you begin to have awakening signs, you are scraping off the dross of this world, meaning the sludge, or things that no longer resonate with your souls' journey. Your soul is destined to return to its original state and place and as it expands in love consciousness it begins to vibrate at a much higher rate. The side effects of that vibration affect the physical body in many ways, especially if we are not conscious of the state of our bodies. This is what we would refer to as the awakening symptoms you may be currently experiencing.

Imagine if your soul had a mind or intelligence of its own -because it does. Imagine if your soul vibrated at the full capacity of its divine intelligence and light, with no thought or care for your physical body. With this accelerated vibration, the genetic makeup of your physical body would not be able to withstand the intensity of the vibration, to the point where your physical body would instantly disintegrate and return to the dust of the earth. Thankfully, your soul knows how to integrate with your body in divine and intelligent ways. As we move into honoring our physical bodies that our souls are housed in, we will then begin a relationship that is destined to become one as we raise to connect with love consciousness.

The relationship that you have with yourself is one of the most important relationships you will ever experience. What is energetically activated internally within you, will also be activated, and experienced externally. Your inner world reflects your outer world. The synergistic relationship you are meant to create between your spiritual body and your physical body is evolving as you make choices that will honor the highest integrity of both.

As we move on, consider what you are creating within the cocoon of your body. What will emerge when you break free from you limiting perceptions or belief systems? What kind of butterfly will push past the walls of doubt, fear, or uncertainty as it transforms through its awakening process? Imagine what you will reflect to the world as you ascend to new ways of thinking, being, and knowing and how that might induce the birthing of other butterflies still wrapped up tightly within their own cocoons.

Chapter 8

The Divine Frequencies of DNA

Imagine if you will, being invited to go into a library of stored energy to experience it as your physical self. It is unlike any library you've ever been in because this incredible library stores the energy and intelligence of all that you are as a divine being. The information stored in this library is infinitely expansive with pixels of numerous vibrating colors, communicating a massively collective expression of the divine intelligence of your soul. The billions upon billions of energetic pixels are very much alive with light frequencies and carry important information for the spiritual makeup of you. You observe the information spanning upward and outward as far as the eye can see, with no apparent shape or form, because you are standing right in the middle of your soul as the physical observer. All together these vibrating pixels of information are one harmonious electrical circuit connecting end to end in the form of multiple strands of spiritual DNA that form the genetic makeup or blueprint of your infinite self. All information was co-created by you and the divine consciousness of all creation through your multiple lifetimes and experiences. Every spiritual gift you have mastered is stored here as well as every positive and negative experience through multiple lifetimes and dimensions, through eternal time, distance, and space. This library represents who you are, where you've been, what you've mastered, what you've enjoyed, what you've resisted and so much more. It encompasses everything and anything about you. Every vibrating pixel carries a massive amount of information about your journey, void of any judgement by you or anyone else who might be privileged to view the library of your infinite blueprint. It is the perfection that humanity has been blind to. It is divine love expressed and illuminated in unconditional form.

When I was a child, I would play for hours with a toy called, "Light Bright." It was a box like structure with many holes in the front of it. As a child, I would push brightly colored pegs into the holes to create a picture. The best part about this toy was plugging it into the wall and watching the pegs light up with all the vibrant colors, bringing the picture to life.

I use this childhood memory as an analogy to paint a picture of our spiritual DNA and how it cooperatively works within our physical body. When our soul is housed in our physical body, certain activated circuits light up within our spiritual DNA structures, creating a picture that can connect with our physical body and the body subsequently responds to each vibrating stimulus now plugged in. Adjusting to such internal phenomena can take time as we have been so conditioned to view the world through our physical eyes, to the point where we are blind to our inner light.

Despite this challenge before us, life has a way of navigating some of us toward our light in sometimes alarming situations. Such was the case of my best friend, Leela. Like myself, she too had gone through the dark night of the soul through her personal life experiences. Much like everyone else, she dreamed of having a great life. She had visions of getting married, starting a family, and expanding upon her business ideas with her entrepreneurial spirit. We all have great intentions, yet life doesn't always turn out the way we've planned it. For her, the path of pain seemed to be chosen by the Gods as her destiny.

Leela married at age 26 and became an instant mother to two amazing children. She adopted them into her heart like any caring mother would. Just one year later she gave birth to her only daughter. All seemed to be going along as planned for the blended family, until a devastating car accident intruded upon her life. While on the way to the hospital, Leela had excruciating pain crushing through her chest wall. She could hardly breathe. At the hospital, unexpected news erupted, echoing into her dazed state. The doctors informed her that they found a football sized tumor over her thymus gland. At that moment, any sense of stability came crashing down around her.

Leela underwent emergency surgery, to what felt like complete exposure of her heart wall to the world. It seemed like the hidden emotions of her vulnerabilities leaked out for all to see and bear witness to. She fell upon complete exposure to the fears she had held in for so long. The silent tumor lodged in her body had much to reveal. Painful emotions surfaced as the tumor was removed. The regrets, the pain, the anger, the doubts, and other strong emotions that could not truly be defined as they flooded in with an unbearable weight on her soul. Just what kind of a soul was she to experience so much?

With the shielding of the tumor now removed, her heart was now free to expand in even more incredibly demanding ways. The experience seemed to create a domino effect of even more trauma, yet to enter her life.

Along with the surgery came more medical news, an autoimmune disease which meant more fear, more uncertainty, and more letting go of what she thought her life was supposed to be. The emotional struggles of life got the best of her and literally bound her body in a gripping cocoon that she couldn't seem to break free of. With the feeling of being paralyzed in a life riddled with fear, Leela suddenly found herself temporarily paralyzed from the neck down. Even with this terrifying event, the dark night of her soul had just begun.

In time, Leela's body continued to spiral downward, sporadically breaking away the physical things that she relied upon for comfort. Her eyesight began to slowly deteriorate. She couldn't bear to watch the pieces of her life break away any further. She was losing her sight, but thankfully, not her will to fight.

Leela recounts that the most painful thing about going blind, was the day that the window of her peripheral vision closed as she caught the last glimpse of her five-year daughter's smile. It would seem it was some type of cruel punishment from unseen forces; however, such was not the case. Although the windows of her physical world were slammed shut, she chose to take the journey into the light of her unlimited soul.

Despite these challenging extremes, Leela became better, not bitter. She is a person who once carried every piece of her life through the dark night and came out emerging from the cocoon, a different person. The closing of the windows to her soul, in no way diminished the light now radiating within her.

Today, Leela often remarks excitedly that she sees an internal light within. It has multiple pileated colors spiraling and expanding through her and all around her. As time moves on and as she now meets the challenges before her with a smile. Her soul is now in the driver's seat, consciously navigating her way through the obstacles of life. As she steps into the heart of courage and faith, she says that the light continues to expand in vibration, color, and sound. The light of this beautifully radiant energy can often be seen by those who pass her by, and they remark just how beautifully captivating and consuming her light is. Unknown to the onlookers, they are drawn to her because she powerfully reflects what is within each of us. She was blind, but now she sees the truth of the I am presence within her.

Leela continues to experience awakening indicators on multiple levels. She is now rebuilding the pieces that she once carried across the threshold of her darkest part of the night. She often giggles as she describes how she feels vibrating energy moving through her body communicating to every single cell now awakening and transforming.

This vibrational shift that many have experienced like Leela, at one time or another during their awakening process can feel rather alarming at first. Be reassured from someone who has experienced it in exponential ways, your spiritual DNA codes are simply communicating with your physical DNA for genetic upgrades now occurring within. With many individuals, just like you, this is the morning alarm now going off. You have slept way too long in the cocoon of your mind and your divine self is urging you to wake up to the light of who you truly are.

Chapter 9

Our Full Divine Expression

These newly channeled concepts we are sharing with you may take some time to digest as you come to integrate these new ways to support you in navigating your way through your personal awakening process. Despite the physical, emotional, mental, and spiritual shifts that are occurring in your life, your physical body and your spiritual body really do desire to have a healthy, symbiotic relationship. A symbiotic relationship is a cooperative relationship between two parties where both are receiving benefits from what each party has to offer. Think of how a butterfly supports the pollination of a flower carrying its lifeforce for further germination. In turn, the butterfly is also sustained by being nourished by the flower. Your physical body houses your spirit, and in return your spiritual body sustains your life here.

When the process of ascension begins to occur the physical and spiritual bodies gradually come together through a higher pre-life soul agreement. Think of a marriage in the earth plain where two individuals make sacred vows to come together as one. What we are explaining here is much the same. Both bodies have agreed to harmoniously merge through a cooperative effort over time. Both hold the awareness that their destiny was always intended to become one body, divinely perfected, awakened, and whole. The two bodies together represent the heavens and earth coming together as one, so we literally create heaven on earth within us. Both bodies carry essential DNA structures for spiritual ascension. One body cannot be the full expression of itself without the other. In relation to the analogy of the butterfly that we have been using throughout this material, the eternal separation of the physical body and the spiritual body, would be like having a butterfly without its wings.

As mentioned before, this process of ascension will not happen for everyone at the same time. Through awakening symptoms, and the casting off of the excess dross from our hearts, humans will begin to merge these two essential bodies together over a period of time. For every soul, the journey takes multiple lifetimes to accomplish. We are coming to a time of ascension where there might only be a handful who may accomplish such a thing during this lifetime, or at least come close, while others will need to incarnate again and again to continue their awakening to the divine relationship between their physical body and their spiritual body. All is in divine timing, order, and purpose. At the same time, we must keep in mind that this process of ascension is not a judgment on an individual. You could compare the learning process to a baby learning to walk. No one would ever consider scolding a baby because they happen to stumble while learning how to master the art of walking. Much is the same for the path of the soul learning to walk a journey of remembering their eternal divinity and destiny. It is a natural developmental progression that we will all naturally master in our own time.

In being true to my path and the things I have been taught through visions, outer body experiences, and teachings from whom I will refer to as ascended masters, and the I Am presence of God, I know that in the places and spaces I have been in the spiritual realms, I have only experienced unconditional love in its perfection. There was no one to judge or condemn me during any times of visitation. All beings have lovingly presented themselves in ways that are impossible to fully describe, however, for the purpose of this material I will openly share one such beautiful experience; one that I remember as an unexpected life review created for the transformation of my soul.

I have had many outer body experiences where my soul has travelled along an energy highway transporting me to spiritual realms that are unseen to the naked eye. One evening as I lay in bed, wrestling with the inner turmoil of my third marriage, I was met with a painful question. "Am I to fail once again?" It would seem that the inevitable answer was right before me, haunting me like all other dark nights of my soul, revolving around the idea of marriage which felt more like suffocating layers of eternal bondage to me. I tossed around the question of choosing physical comforts of security or my spiritual expression and freedom to expand into the unknown paths of my soul. I quickly uttered a solemn prayer that was bathed in helplessness, with no real energy to even hear the answer. I was exhausted by my life and the efforts it took to remain fully present here. After some time of silence, nothing was coming to me or through me in the way of inspiration. It seemed as if the heavens were not speaking to me, leaving me to drown in my own silence of countless stinging tears. I was clearly clouded in my ability to hear the answer as I lay emotionally disoriented before falling asleep.

During sometime through the heavy darkness of what seemed to be a sleepless night, I was instantly transported beyond the awareness of my physical body. In a somewhat of a disoriented condition, I found myself surrounded by an intelligent white light in a heavenly realm or what I will refer to as a space between worlds. I had been brought there before, however, this time it felt different. I was now experiencing this peaceful space as if it were the very breath of divine love securely holding me in its presence. Initially, I found myself alone, yet unafraid, and open to whatever the experience was meant to teach me. I began a meditational prayer of the heart to inquire about the purpose of the occasion. Within seconds of my pure thought, the one known as Jesus, lightly descended in front of me. His illuminated presence enveloped me with such a loving and compassionate embrace that has been etched within my soul forever. I knew he knew me deeply and intimately as we were eternally connected heart to heart, soul to soul. His presence was captivating and his radiance, indescribably brilliant. His eyes were like crystals filled with a piercing love that penetrated my being, connecting us on levels that I cannot clearly explain through mere words. There was a telepathic communication that built a bridge of complete unity and a sense oneness between us, a knowingness deep within my soul. Within what seemed like a noticeably short period of time, my earth life was presented in a panoramic view within a one second flash of insight. I understood and processed the vision instantaneously and in my fragmented state as a soul, a heaviness then fell upon me. The burden of earths illusion encompassed my entire being and I fell helplessly to my knees weeping what felt like a million tears. In that moment, I was shown that the choices I had made through life created consequential earth experiences that were far beneath my gifts and potential as a divine being. In that moment, I felt as if I had failed on many levels, yet in the eyes of the one who observed me, there was no such thing as failure. The only thing this beautiful being saw in me was the unlimited potential to be the presence of love. In that moment of heaviness, he requested if he could lift the veil of forgetfulness from my eyes, freeing me from my own imprisonment of judgment. My love for this beautiful being was so great, I first hesitated, for I did not wish for him to feel the burden of my earthy choices.

Yet, the love was so all encompassing and consuming, I agreed with the sincerest humility. An unforgettable miracle occurred in that divine moment. The weight was lifted, and a transference of beautiful divine energy moved through my being like waves of heavenly purification. It felt like a baptism of sorts, a baptism of my heart. I understand now that Jesus, the one who had mastered the art of unconditional love, showed up as a mirror for me in that moment to show what was possible for all of us. It was truly a gift of divine intervention.

In sharing this experience with you, I wish you to understand that this experience is not shared through any religious affiliations or belief systems related to mankind's interpretation of Jesus. I have met other ascended beings much like Jesus who have been Christed or anointed with the I Am presence of God or what we call divine love. Jesus had accomplished what we have been referring to in this material. He had become master over his body and his soul, merging them together as one divine body that we call ascension.

Your belief systems are simply that - your belief systems. They are a beautiful part of your journey and your personal experience in the earth plain. As mentioned before, you did not come here with your belief systems. You adopted your belief systems by the influence of others who have told you what to believe. We are not telling you what to believe or even how to be. That is your journey to master.

For now, my sincere hope is that the beautiful transference of healing energy that I once received, would be transferred to you as well. Treat yourself as you would a child who is learning to navigate their way through life. Extend patience to yourself and encourage yourself to get back up if you feel you have stumbled along the way.

Chapter 10

The God Code

We've been emphasizing the communion between your physical body and your spiritual body to prepare you to receive the information now being channeled about humanity's divine ascension. This information is for the purposes of your awareness, yet not necessary for you to adopt as your own personal belief systems in order to learn of your awakening signs and how to navigate your way through them.

Much like myself, there are many individuals who have miraculously transformed former dysfunctional behaviors into creating a miraculous and mighty change of heart. Going from disillusioned prisoner to a contributing member of society can occur, yet we often close our hearts off to such things. If we are unforgiving of ourselves, chances are we will be unforgiving of others. Where are you in your life? In what ways have you imprisoned yourself? Have you imprisoned yourself with guilt or shame and thrown away the key or have you given someone else control of the key? No matter where you may find yourself in this moment, don't lose heart. You can have a mighty change of heart and break free of the things that have kept you from awakening to your grand ascension.

In referring to such, consider for a moment that our hearts have the ability to be energetically soften or harden. They can be energetically open or energetically closed depending on our interpretation and integration of our life's experiences.

For example, a person with a hardened, closed off heart might exhibit hard behaviors such as judgment, bitterness, resentment, anger, and hatefulness. This person represents someone whose heart isn't in full communion or communication with their soul, or the I Am presence of God, due to trauma or life experiences that may have left them feeling guarded. A person who has an open heart, energetically soft and pliable, will often show behaviors such as compassion, kindness, empathy, understanding and love. This person represents someone whose heart is gradually learning to be in communion or communication with their soul, or the I Am presence of God, through their earth experiences. Keep in mind our hearts can at times be opened or closed to our various interpretations of life.

Let's look at the heart from a different angle. You may be familiar with the saying, "Be still and know that I am God?" Why stillness? What can we know in stillness? What can we hear in stillness? What can we orchestrate in stillness? What can be heard when we turn away from the noise and distractions of the world? What can we knowingly hear inside of us? What is being communicated between our physical body and our spiritual body as we live our lives and expand our inner awareness?

In the stillness we can know that the merging of our two bodies gradually ascending are actually created through highly resonating vibrational sounds we will symbolically reference as, "The Light Frequencies of The God Code." The direct communication between these divinely intelligent light frequencies radiates between the energy pulses of our physical hearts, coupled with the vibrational light frequencies radiating from our souls.

We can demonstrate the relationship between sound and physical creation through a simple scientific study known as cymatics. Cymatics is the study of sound waves expressed through vibration and their ability to communicate their vibrational intelligence into the creation of physical form. An example of a cymatics experiment that I witnessed was the following.

A solid metal plate lays flat. It is then sprinkled with a fair bit of sand on its smooth surface. A clamp with a wire is attached to the metal plate which then extends to a speaker. When sound or pitch is played, it is transmitted through the wire to the mental plate. Astoundingly, the sand will begin to move and respond to the pitch of the sound played. The amazing results are not just the fact that the sand moves through the transference of vibration, but that something unexplainable happens. There appears to be an unknown intelligence communicating between sound and sand. Depending on the pitch of sound played, various geometrical patterns and shapes are formed by the sand dancing across the steel surface. It is absolutely astounding to watch!

Given this information, imagine your soul now representing the voice of the I Am presence of the God within, divinely speaking to the surface of your physical heart. Imagine the expansively beautiful healing patterns being created within your physical body right now.

Chapter 11

Resurrecting Your Cellular Memory

Let's return to the library we talked about earlier. The DNA structures of the spiritual body or that infinite library. This encompasses the intrinsic light frequencies of the souls' experiences through many interdimensional paths, from lifetime to lifetime, building upon its structure to eventually experience itself as the I Am Presence of Love. In turn, the physical body encompasses the genetic makeup of the physical DNA structures which are encoded through our multiple earth life experiences. These life experiences hold the memories of emotion, or e-motion, in other words, energy in-motion being expressed through physical form. These emotions, both positive and negative, are passed down from lifetime to lifetime, and also from generation to generation.

The idea of multiple incarnations on earth may be a new concept for you to consider. There was a time where such knowledge was foreign to me as well, yet through my personal experiences, I have since integrated this knowing of incarnations into my heart.

There have been many case studies where young children have been able to recall the finite details about their past lives right down to family members, their life experiences, their language, and how they specifically died. Through detailed and extensive investigation, it has been found that the information these children provided were remarkably affirmed. For children, the veil of the physical body is very thin, so some are able to recall past lives. For them, the memories can be so incredibly vivid, they could be compared to looking back into another room they had recently left. There are also people who have experienced hypnotherapy who have had no former belief systems revolving around past lives. When undergoing hypnosis, they have surprisingly been awakened to the fact that some of their emotional upset or instability in their current life was due to an unresolved past life experience. As we awaken, both body and soul are on a journey of remembering the truth within. I would encourage you to investigate such things for yourself. It may lead you to the uncharted corridors of your journey, supporting you in your awakening process.

With every incarnation, the spiritual body brings with it the memories of its countless experiential existences. In essence it brings a whole library of memories with it. We mentioned earlier that the information stored in this library holds infinitely expansive pixelated light frequencies that carry the information of your soul. Some in the spiritual community refer to this library as the akashic records. As our souls live, they expand and build upon the information in our akashic records. This is a unique blueprint of our co-creation with the I Am presence within us. For lack of a better comparison, our souls are in essence, like an extremely complicated computer system communicating simultaneously with both the physical and spiritual realms. As our souls build upon their library systems life after life, they increase in light frequency and of course spiritual mastery.

We can see the evidence of this in recent years. It is undeniable that we have seen some incredibly old souls that we view as children, entering the planet with their highly intuitive and spiritual gifts in tack. They are in fact arriving spiritually awake with much of their library of light pixels already activated within their souls. These children tend to speak wisdom beyond their years, have unexplained gifts that are completely developed and can see through the illusions and conditioning of the world. Perhaps you know of such a child. Some have referred to these children as indigo, crystal, or rainbow children.

Depending on the activation of the light frequencies with our soul, the physical body will be affected differently. I'm sure you have heard the phrase, *"The eyes are the windows to the soul."* In a person whose soul is resonating with high light frequencies, that light can actually be seen through their eyes or in their countenance and can also be felt by their physical presence. Often times people will remark how a pregnant woman is glowing. That glow comes from the pure soul that has not yet come into the world, for in the womb unborn souls hold the pure expression of divine love before entering into the deep conditioning of the physical world.

In addition to this, and as another example, it has been shown that electromagnetic imaging will also reflect the illumination of colors within a person's aura in association with their chakras or energy centers of the body. Although this is fun to view, the complete image of the chakras or aura could be referenced as one grain of sand when compared to the magnificent image of the infinite soul. If you are not familiar with the chakras, I invite you to explore the chakras and their purposes through my online course which can be found at: *courses.heartcenteredreiki.org*

Lifetime after lifetime we are upgrading the integration between spiritual soul and physical body. We rebirth the intelligence of the soul and as we do, we experience what we will refer to as birthing pains within the physical body. As a soul and physical body communicate through the vibration of the heart and the light frequencies of the soul, one is naturally induced to rebirth its perception of self. Through this process, it is then that the awakening symptoms begin. These contractions push out any aspect of individual limitation or division that are often anchored in our emotions of attachment throughout our physical perceptions of life.

As the spiritual soul continues to raise in consciousness by connecting to the I Am presence of love, it directly affects the physical DNA and cell structures of the body. The two bodies are intrinsically now seeking to merge as one conscious being through the energies and experience of acceptance, forgiveness, compassion, empathy, and love. They no longer oppose one another internally or externally. Through this process of complete and harmonious reconciliation, the two bodies will eventually become one, the heavens and the earth meet, no longer being divided. A divine marriage is celebrated. A new body is formed, having accomplished its divine assignment, pre-life contract, and destiny of spiritual mastery and ascension. Divine love will now be experienced in perfect form through the I Am presence of God ascending.

Chapter 12

Your Family Tree

How conscious are we willing to go as we go about our daily activities in our awakening process? How far are we willing to open the expansive corridors of our heart, allowing it to integrate with the divine intelligence of our soul? How can we bridge the gap of conflict between our mind and heart to support us in our awakening process? These questions must be addressed both individually and collectively.

The way we can know the answers to these pertinent questions, first individually, then collectively, is by pure observation. Much like how we brought you to observe the internal world of your infinite library of your soul, we can now also direct your infinite soul to observe the physical plain of the external world. Understand that the foundational layer of the physical world first begins with our physical body. This is the closest physical thing that our soul can observe, yet most are tempted to look past their physical body, into a world of physical things.

When the integration of our physical and spiritual bodies are incomplete, in other words, not in full communion as one ascended being, we carry glitches or short circuits within both of our systems. Even though we may have some short circuits showing up in some areas of our soul body and physical body, it doesn't mean that all circuits are broken.

A great analogy to demonstrate this is by imagining a string of lights ready to be strung on a Christmas tree. This string of lights I am referring to is an incredibly old string of lights that have been passed down from generation to generation, and now they have been passed down to you. They are somewhat of an heirloom, priceless, and most definitely irreplaceable. In fact, they are so old, the replacement bulbs are no longer available for purchase. As you carefully line the tree with the lights, you make sure that every tree limb is covered and then the moment arrives where it's time to light up the tree. You insert the plug into the outlet with great anticipation because it's finally your turn to experience seeing the beautiful array of heirloom lights, yet you are met with the unexpected. Some areas of the tree, beam with and array of brilliant colors, while you notice sporadic areas where various bulbs have blown a fuse. In an attempt to salvage the look and feel of the ambience of the tree, you quickly tuck the burnt-out bulbs under the branches hoping that no one will notice. The problem is this act places even more demand on the main circuit as it has to work harder to move the electrical current through the burn out bulbs to the bulbs that are functioning properly. As a result, some areas of the tree are lit up with energy, while other areas are energetically dormant.

Are you getting the picture? Your physical and spiritual bodies are much like this Christmas tree we described. The tree represents your physical body, while the string of lights represents your soul body. There are hidden areas of your body that remain in darkness or are energetically dormant. This is where the beginning of dis-ease quietly spreads, despite your attempts to hide it.

So, one may have the question, "Why were the lights not in perfect condition when you received them?" After all, to your knowledge it was your very first time you had ever laid eyes on them, or so you might think. Let's look at a symbolic picture in continuing to paint the picture of your family tree.

In your multiple lifetimes, or even through this current lifetime, there may have been times where you weren't paying attention to your tree's lighting system because you were so distracted by the external world filled with trees much like yourself. You may have seen a tree with more vibrant colors than yours and perhaps jealousy entered into your circuitry system. Or perhaps someone stole one of your bulbs and anger entered into your circuitry system. In fact, you've spent so much of your time and energy judging all the other trees around you that your circuitry system became energetically drained.

Let's face it, we have a connection and a relationship with the external world, yet when we place our energy there, and become entangled with emotions such as hate, jealousy, revenge, envy, regret, shame, blame, or any other glitches that would enter into our personal circuitry system, we will encounter what we call health issues. In this, we have disconnected from the circuitry of our soul and if not attended to and cared for it gets carried over into our soul's library of circuitry lifetime after lifetime. Disease occurs when our physical and spiritual bodies are not fully integrated or communing as one body. This is why we eventually all experience what we call death, yet even in death, there is hope. Most in life, fear death. It is a topic that is seldom talked about, that is, until it stares us right in the face. A loved one is dying or has died, or perhaps you are suddenly faced with your own mortality.

Death is in essence a spiritual rebirth where a soul releases itself from the body, much like a butterfly releases itself from their cocoon. The temporary body has served its purpose as a vehicle during a lifetime for the soul's expansive growth and expression. A butterfly does not mourn the loss of its cocoon, nor should we mourn the loss of a body if it has not yet reached the level of ultimate ascension. In the physical world, it appears as if something has been lost, yet in truth, nothing has been lost as the soul is as bright and as brilliant and alive as it ever was long after leaving the body. Many individuals who have had near death experiences recount the peace and freedom their soul felt after leaving their cumbersome bodies and most were reluctant to return.

The good news is, we are given infinite opportunities to connect and reconnect with a body, lifetime after lifetime until a completely divine integration of body and soul are accomplished. Keep in mind that although it may feel like you are starting over, you are not. With every lifetime a soul brings in all memories from all lifetimes, amplifying and building upon its spiritual DNA, which will then connect and integrate with a new physical body. The whole process is divinely orchestrated, so no matter how badly you may think you've messed up in a lifetime, just know that nothing you have ever experienced is in vain. All experiences are for the benefit of your spiritual awareness and awakening which are clearly pointing you to your eventual ascension. We are indeed ascending, individually, and collectively. In doing so, we must trust that our family tree is becoming stronger as our spiritual and physical roots connect on deeper levels.

Chapter 13

Our Conscious Observations

Now that we have created a visual reference for you, in the previous chapter, let's bring your attention to observing your physical body. As the infinite soul that you are, housed in your body, pay attention to what energies seem to flow through your heart without any resistance. Your physical heart acts as the battery connected to the circuitry of your soul's library. Imagine your heart plugged into your soul, lighting up all of the pixelated colors of your circuitry system. Typically, natural light energies that can flow freely through your heart may be emotions like joy, excitement, kindness, compassion, love, connection, and empathy.

Think of the last time you did something to induce these beautiful feelings. Perhaps it was a time where you made an unexpected visit to someone who was feeling ill, or when you smiled at a stranger, or when you gave a birthday gift to a child. We've all had these elated feelings at one time or another. They seem to stay with us, years after the uplifting experience occurred. These emotions of high vibration and expansion literally fuel your soul body and physical body. This refueling reactivates the connections between the physical DNA and the spiritual DNA charging them with the frequencies of connection, regeneration, and healing. The once energetically dormant areas within both bodies can be resurrected by attending to the fundamental and foundational layers of you. Choosing to live in highly vibrational states of emotions, expands our awareness and awakening journey, thus allowing for the birthing pains associated with awakening to be mastered with greater ease and grace.

We would now ask that you observe the things in the external world. The external world appears to be on the outside of you and is where your analytical mind tends to trip on things that are merely a false reflection of who you are.

Let's take you on a trip to an amusement park to explain what we wish to convey. In this amusement park we will display a variety of mirrors purposely designed to distort your physical image. First, see yourself standing in front of a wavy mirror. You'll notice that your body appears to be wavy. Now, see yourself standing in front of a wide mirror and you'll now notice that your body appears to be wide. Finally, see yourself standing in front of a narrow mirror. Do you see what I see? That's right, your body appears to be narrow. These mirrors of amusement are merely a false reflection of you. You'll note as you look at your real body void of the mirror reflecting back at you that it is the same as what it has always been. This amusement park of mirrors is also what the external world tries to reflect back to you when you find yourself being absorbed by all the distortions and illusions tripping your mind. This reflection creates an energy of resistance because the divine intelligence of your soul body understands that these things outside of you are not you. This observation of external trickery will often move the mind into the energy of resistance.

As mentioned in an earlier chapter, the energy of resistance can encompass emotions such as judgement, anger, hatred, jealousy, envy, shame, blame, regret, and many others. These emotions consciously and unconsciously drain the energy of the heart. Think of a time when you became angry with someone. Maybe it was through an act of deep betrayal, or perhaps the anger erupted when someone cut you off while driving, or perhaps the anger has festered within you for so long you can't even pinpoint an actual occasion. You only know you feel dark inside and your anger makes you even more angry.

Negative energy depletes the heart's battery that was divinely designed to orchestrate and integrate the complete connection of your soul body with your physical body. Through the entanglement of these negative energies into your circuitry system, your soul body and physical body begin to show symptoms of dis-ease between both bodies. The divine communion has been interrupted. In time, with these negative energies coursing through your circuitry system, the once brilliantly pixelated colors within your soul's library begin to glitch and become distorted energy. Distorted energy is simply energy that has no framework, or clear energy pathway of connection. Certain areas along the multiple strands of your spiritual DNA, begin to turn dim, thus interrupting the once clear connection between points of internal communication. In time, if there is not a recharge in the hearts regulatory system, through a mighty change of heart, some of the spiritual pixels will burnt out altogether, much like the Christmas tree lights we referred to before. Choosing to engage in negative vibrational states of emotions disrupts our soul/body connection.

The journey of conscious observation can be mastered by the way we choose to interpret our internal connection between our soul body and physical body. We have everything we need to heal within, and yet the external world of illusionary mirrors will reflect what we expect to see, experience and be. As we learn to establish a relationship rooted in the emotions of love consciousness, that beautifully alive and intelligent energy will fuel the heart instead of depleting it of its life force. As our heart is fueled, our intricate internal circuitries of DNA, both spiritual and physical, will be activated into a new way of experiencing ourselves. With this conscious activation we invite what humans call miracles to be fully and authentically experienced on every conceivable level. What some have emphatically once stated as impossible, will now be possible.

This is the ultimate journey of the human race. The pathway of ascension has been revealed and is now before you. Your soul calls you to rise to that pinnacle of truth that you have always known within.

"Life is an intricate puzzle of potential and you, dear friend, are a part of that infinite puzzle of possibilities. What piece will you be today in the picture of one heart now awakening?"
- Leslie Paramore

Chapter 14

The Death of You

The way we can know we are successfully moving through the birthing pains of awakening is by observing what is showing up in our panoramic view both internally and externally, from sunrise to sunset and everything in between. Our awakening process even continues as we sleep, as we drift off into another dream world to sort out the rough edges of our unconscious mind.

In using the analogy of the butterfly in this material we have mentioned the journey of the butterfly eventually emerging from its cocoon, yet before this can happen, a death of the old must first occur. The caterpillar must let go of ways of being in order to transform. Its old body is broken down with secretive juices and it literally digests itself from the inside out. As the fluid breaks down the old body, new cells are formed. Through this natural process of letting go, a newly elevated expression of life is created through this beautiful resurrection.

What part of us is willing to die? As we go through our awakening process, we are going through a death of sorts . . . the death of the old parts of us. We cannot take the old parts of us to where we are going, no more than a butterfly can carry the old shadows of the cocoon on its back. Imagine how that would hinder the spread of its marvelous wings now ready to take flight. Just as the butterfly, through our awakening process, we must also be willing to let go of the cocoon of old belief systems that have kept our heart in the shadows of doubt and fear.

The feeling that we are literally dying can be a very real feeling through this process known as awakening. We are in fact awakening multiple layers of our complete being which include the layers of emotional, mental, physical, and spiritual intelligences. As we work through these layers, we will experience various symptoms or sensations, although as mentioned before not everyone will experience the same sensations in the same way, or for the same time periods. Let's briefly outline the four bodies to offer examples of how these can be affected during our awakening process.

Let's start with our emotions. During our awakening, walls of unresolved emotion within our heart finally break down and crumble, leaving our once buried feelings exposed to the elements; raw, real, and vulnerable. Everyone will experience this differently. Some may literally experience a nervous breakdown, while others may have the occasional moody day, and if not attended to these can create a domino effect, cascading into things such as depression, anxiety and other awakening symptoms that can leave us feeling emotionally unsettled. Oftentimes we may even think we are going crazy, and these experiences may try to become a part of our personified beliefs about ourselves. The important thing to remember no matter what is showing up, on a higher level, you know exactly what you are doing.

As we address the mental aspect of our body, the mental walls of worldly conditioning must also come down. In this, we are called to release the fears of the false ego, detaching from the illusionary power of the external world. This means no longer allowing things that once triggered us to spiral downward into negative emotions. We are instead being called to invite the divine mind of the infinite self to integrate its energy within our circuitry systems of our physical and spiritual body.

Ultimately with this integration of mind, body, and spirit, we can now communicate clearly as one divine body. Think of this integration as the perfect triangle of communication, completely balanced and whole. In this shift we are unplugging our personal perceptions of the physical matrix and instead going inward to reestablish a foundational relationship with the divine mind of the I Am presence within.

In the awakening process we are also invited to elevate our physical bodies to the highest degree possible in any given lifetime. The physical body learns to move into higher frequencies of being and understanding what is truly possible. We come to learn how to honor and master the physical body to a new level. We in essence are learning to resurrect ourselves, just as the one we know as Jesus resurrected himself. Through this process, or co-creating shifts within our Physical DNA we are crossing boundaries unknown to mankind. We may experience uncomfortable sensations as negative energies work their way out of the physical circuitry of cells.

As a simple analogy, imagine negative energy in our physical body as a long-barbed sliver embedded in our flesh. It has pierced our body and anchored itself there for so long, that it has festered into an energetic infection. As the energy of infection oozes its way out of our physical body, it can be quite uncomfortable. Hence the unexplainable aches and pains that we have from time to time. If the energetic slivers stay within our bodies, then dis-ease occurs due to the breakages within our circuitry systems. In our awakening, some may experience physical indicators to one degree or another. I have found the most powerful way to ease any physical discomfort is through the power of gratitude. I am just touching on the powerful energy of gratitude right now, however, we will explain more about this way of being later on.

And finally, we address the spiritual layers that are a part of our body systems. In this shift there are many who will move from atheist to believer, from religious to spiritual, from agnostic to pagan, and so on. Sometimes an individual will go through many shifts to get to a space of contentment, and then continue on further to gradual spiritual expansion and awareness of the soul that is housed within. Shifts in belief systems can feel like a death especially if those belief systems have been ingrained in us since birth. We are essentially leaving the tribal traditions or social conditionings and uprooting from everything we were ever taught. This shift can be painfully riddled with feelings of shame, guilt, and secrecy on our part for fear of disappointing those we love. Leaving our tribal traditions can feel like we are leaving our loved ones behind by severing the once adopted belief systems that we faithfully and obediently lived in exchange for the acceptance from our tribal family. It can leave us with feelings of exclusion, as we have severed our portion of the branch from our family tree. We are now an orphan or so it may seem. Don't lose heart. In this shift, you are simply finding your way back to the inner heart that has been calling you to come home.

Through our awakening process, individually and collectively, we must get lost in order to be found. We must detach from everything we once knew as truth in order to reconnect the most authentic parts of ourselves. We must go inside like the butterfly, allowing our old systems to be broken down piece by piece until we lose any idea of limitation. Yes, our four bodies will most definitely experience what can feel like a death that will bring us through an unforgettable transformation, just like the butterfly. This transformation is one we can no longer ignore as the vibrations of our bodies push us through our individual and collective transformation. The contraction pains of birthing our true selves is moving us into what we were always meant to be, a conscious being, with a new body integrated as one.

Chapter 15

A Vibrational Shift

The foundational knowledge we are sharing within this material will support you in a deeper understanding of what is actually happening to us individually and collectively. It will actually offer a reference to go to when experiencing the sometimes-unpredictable awakening shifts being experienced to one degree or another. The information offered here will leave you feeling much more at ease and more able to confidently adapt to what shows up in your life. Yes, as we have been exploring, there is a vibrational shift going on with this planet and also, within you.

The earth's vibrational resonance has been measured in its natural state of 7.83 Hertz, however, in recent years, as early as 2017 the frequencies of the earth have shifted to an extra 15 to 25 hertz. In obtaining this new awareness, what exactly does this mean for us? Science has shown that the higher the frequency, the more energetic information can be transferred or shared. Since we are connected to the earth both physically and energetically, we can naturally conclude that similar shifts are also occurring within us. The question is to what degree of frequency elevation are we going and are we ready for the shift? We could go into the deep scientific studies here, however, it is sufficient to note that we are shifting to higher frequencies right along with this planet.

Just as your spiritual body is plugged into your physical body, along with the activation of your divine mind, imagine now being plugged into the frequencies of the earth and what that means. A simple yet beautiful reference we can look to when these circuit systems are in balance is by observing a natural phenomenon that occurs in nature.

A wonderful reference in nature is when we see the starlings moving beautifully to the collective consciousness of one. The resonating frequencies of their essence or lifeforce is connected internally as well as externally. It would appear that each starling sees the other starlings around it as an extended version of itself. They vibrate harmoniously, and therefore, they move together in unison. When one turns in a particular direction, they all move in that direction, painting a beautiful synchronistic dance across the sky's canvas. It creates a view of one lifeforce moving intelligently as if they were being communicated with by something outside of themselves.

Individuals have often been told that animals communicate through some innate instinct, however, we are asking you to consider that perhaps animals communicate through telepathy which is the ability to tap into high frequency sound waves between two or more life forces.

In continuing to demonstrate this concept of telepathic connection, animals have often been known to run to higher ground long before a disaster like a tsunami reaches the shorelines, whereas humans strolling along the shoreline are left completely unaware of the impending doom. In one such case, a friend of mine mentioned a personal experience he had while in Texas 1967. Within just a couple of days, Hurricane Bula found its way sweeping through Texas, he witnessed a mass migration of various animals moving inland. Turtles, armadillos, insects, birds and some other wildlife intuitively made their way along the highway, moving conscientiously to the safety of higher ground. It was quite an unusual occurrence to bear witness to.

What are the animals tapped into that our human beings are not? Who or what is communicating with the animals? In investigating these questions, we would suggest that animals have a direct connection and communion with the earth, plugging into her intelligent frequencies of the silent soundwaves of direct communication.

In our awakening process we would suggest that there is great support in connecting with and communing with the earth. We would again ask you to imagine what a difference that could mean in your awakening process. Plugging in your circuitry systems by grounding into her soil might very well offer you much more than you may realize. What potential nourishment and communication could we also receive by consciously connecting to the earth's natural frequencies? Let's plug into the next chapter and find out.

Chapter 16

Navigating Ourselves into Awareness

In the next few segments of this channeled material, we will be focusing on some of the indicators that could point the way to your ultimate spiritual awakening. We will first outline what the indicator is, and how it might be showing up in your life. As mentioned before, not everyone experiences every symptom or indicator to the same degree. Another thing to keep in mind as you go through this material is that there may be an awakening indicator that you have not yet experienced or may never experience. Remember that your soul knows exactly how to navigate you through the birthing of the real you.

After outlining the indicator, we will then move into sharing the possibilities of why this symptom may be showing up to support you in making sense of the unexplained. The main reason that I was led to create this material is because I have witnessed many individuals going through experiences that make them feel like they are losing their minds as no one can explain the disruption that has interrupted their lives. From personal experience I know how uncomfortable this can feel, however, let me reassure you that you are not alone in your awakening process. There are many who are experiencing countless shifts in their lives. Take great comfort that you are divinely supported through these birthing pains of ascension.

And finally, after outlining possible explanations of why this awakening symptom may be occurring in your life, we will then support you with tools to help you to navigate your way through them in the most comfortable way possible. The main thing I would highly recommend as you implement these tools, is to be consistent and do your best to be in a state of nonresistance. As you step into complete acceptance, for the experience it will be much easier for you to move through it.

A simple analogy for you to consider as you go through these experiences is to imagine your higher self, acting as a birthing coach as you give birth to the new you. I think you would agree that your higher self would naturally tell you to relax, and to breathe through the contractions of change which are now occurring in your life. For the purpose of this material, we will refer to a contraction as a shift that is occurring within your life, emotionally, mentally, spiritually, or physically, to bring about greater spiritual awareness. And with this new awareness, you will be able to step into complete acceptance and gratitude for the opportunity to awaken to a new version of you. Imagine rebirthing yourself to a new version of you. Imagine leaving behind those things in your life which have felt heavy or binding. Imagine being free to be what you came to be as a soul, fully aligned in your purpose and your life's path. Imagine having the veil removed from your eyes, now seeing perfectly into the perfection of your journey. Imagine embracing the birthing up the greatest expression of who you are. Just imagine it happening right now.

Mantra: "I AM now awakening to the deeper parts of myself, birthing the divine light of truth through the breath of God within."

Chapter 17

Indicator 1 - Unchanneled Energy

There are many who are experiencing new levels of anxiety. Your first inclination may be to freak out and run to the nearest doctor because you may feel a shaking inside of you with some sensations of overwhelming anxiety for no apparent reason. This energized feeling can come on suddenly, and with no warning, creating a feeling of panic within your circuitry systems, emotionally, physically, mentally, and spiritually.

If you are experiencing this indicator of awakening be reassured, that you can and will get through it. This overloading of repressed emotion must find its way to the surface to be released, and it can be helpful if you give it permission to do so. This repressed emotional energy may have originally rooted itself in childhood trauma not healed and may have continued to build into your adult experiences. In addition, and on a deeper level, the energy could also be ancestral energy that you may have agreed to carry and heal on behalf of your ancestors. Either way, it is best not to overthink or focus on such things as far as the origin, as this can often magnify the energy in question. What would be most beneficial for you is to simply trust that the energies surfacing are long past due and are ready to be compassionately released with your permission.

This over stimulation of energy you may be feeling in the way of shaking or anxiety is an energetic release of the root chakra erupting. In this experience, you are in essence being uprooted from the old energies that can no longer live within you, as you rise in spiritual consciousness through your awakening. Although this energy can be startling, be reassured that the excess energy is simply trying to find its way out of your body's blocked circuitry systems. Your spiritual body is shaking things up to wake things up. You've simply outgrown your limited space in the root chakra which encompasses the survival energy of the third dimensional plane. Now it's time to be energetically planted within your heart, where a new life of thriving awaits you.

Many, like yourself, are feeling the rising energy shifts of this planet. Internally, it can feel chaotic or unsettling because the planet is also shifting frequencies to higher vibrations of ascension and like it or not, so are you. It is important to clarify that there is nothing "wrong" with you. Your body is raising its energetic frequencies to match the frequencies of your soul connection to this planet. Thankfully, there are ways to balance the excess energy by redirecting it. To move you through this as quickly as possible, we will outline some helpful suggestions for you in this material that you can easily integrate into your life. Do those that resonate with you and also remember to tune into yourself and ask what other things could potentially support you through this process.

Chapter 18

Balancing
Unchanneled Energy

With all the energy you may have been feeling, there are some practical and easy things that you can do to encourage the energy to become more balanced and less chaotic within your body. Some of these suggestions you can do daily, however, initially, be sure to step into the ones that resonate with you so that you can ensure success. The more tips you can implement into your life, the more balanced you will become. We offer you the following suggestions:

1. Thrive And Exercise: Exercise daily to move the energy through you. Walk, dance, run, jump, swim, bike, or anything that involves some form of movement for your physical body. Although at first glance, it may appear that exercise would increase your energy, it can directly support the outward channeling of the excess energy you once carried within you.

2. Affirm The Movement: As you move your body, use positive affirmations or mantras in conjunction with the movement. These are simply positive statements that you will create to support your belief systems or thoughts about your experience. Many are aware that it has been shown through medical studies that our belief systems can directly affect how

our body responds to us. For instance, patients unknowingly given a sugar pill or placebo instead of real medication, have been shown great improvement merely by their beliefs. Now, getting back to the idea of using affirmations, it is suggested that you create your own because your body understands your language and is specifically attuned to the forming and frequencies of your thoughts. A couple of examples for reference would be: "Pure energy flows through me calmly and effortlessly." Or "I am a powerful being, now creating balance in my body." Keep in mind that, our minds are powerful tools that our body believes as we channel thoughts through ourselves. When we speak or think calm thoughts, our body can learn to respond to those thoughts, just as easily as you are now responding to this material presented to you.

3. Rest Your Digestion: As you move toward calming and directing the excess energy within your body, you would benefit from eating several balanced small meals throughout the day. Integrating small food portions every three to four to hours will redirect the excess energy toward your digestion. When you balance your meals into smaller portions of food, you balance your body and also, this new practice will assimilate calmer energy needed for proper digestion. Smaller meals are easier to process, creating less stress within your body, placing it into a more relaxed state. In contrast, when you eat larger meals, it places your body into an overdrive state, which causes digestive stress. Digesting large amounts of food overloads your digestive system with too much energy that is eventually stored as an unnecessary excess of fat on your physical body. If you are truthful with yourself, you will agree that excess weight is connected to all aspects of who you are, physically, emotionally, spiritually, and mentally. As you now begin to easily integrate smaller food portions more often, you will find that this action redirects the excess energy you once felt. You will be

amazed at how the simple process of the awareness of digestion will create an energy of relaxation and a more balanced relationship with food.

4. Hydrate Your Body: In continuing to support you through
the excess energy that you may have been feeling we would
also recommend drinking four to six glasses of pure water per
day to support the natural flow of hydration that is needed to
support your body's river systems of energy. When you suf-
ficiently hydrate, you expand the capacity of energy within
your body, which supports your body's ability to perform in
a healthy and balanced manner. We can look at water as a
great conductor or communicator of energy that supports your
body's natural energetic flow through your cells, tissues, and
organs. Water supports your body in a vibratory communication on all levels, so instead of reaching for the soft drinks
filled with stimulating caffeine and addictive chemicals, gravitate to the natural source that was intended to be a part of
your body. As an additional note, it has been shown scientif-
ically, that water holds molecular memory. Along with drinking the water, you can also imprint the water with positive
thoughts before drinking it. If this concept of molecular memory is something you would like to investigate further, I would
highly recommend becoming familiar with Dr. Masaru Emoto's
work, "The Hidden Messages in Water," which can be watched
for free on You Tube.

5. Meditate For Relaxation: There are many ways you can
support your body through these vibrational shifts of energy.
It can be helpful to induce a relaxed state by listening to and
participating in guided meditations, which are designed to balance the mind, body, spirit connection. If you've never par-
ticipated in a guided meditation, it is simply a specifically
designed dialogue often accompanied with music where the

participant is guided into a relaxed state to move stagnant or blocked energy within the mind, body, and spirit. Your job is simply to place yourself in a space free of distraction, in a comfortable position and in a place of openness to receive. I have many guided meditations available on You Tube where you can enjoy the results while you are awake or asleep. Simply go to, "Mindful Meditations - Heart Centered Reiki," to begin your relaxing journey with guided meditations created just for you.

6. Stretch Your Body: In addition to guided meditations, you can also practice simple yoga or stretching to get your energy going and flowing. You might think that this suggestion sounds too simple or maybe even too good to be true, however, being a licensed massage therapist and energy practitioner, I can share a simple analogy with you that I often share with clients who come to me with aches and pains in their bodies.
In this analogy I'm mentioning, I will tell clients how their bodies are kind of like a slinky. Now, to make you aware, a slinky is a long toy made out of circular plastic or wire that can expand or contract depending on how we move it from side to side. In a funny sort of way, all bodies are like a slinky. Just like my clients, your body can also be compressed or expanded depending on movement or non-movement. For instance, if you rarely stretch or move, your physical body can quickly become compressed and restricted like a tightly closed slinky. On the other hand, when you take time to stretch or move your body, you are in essence stretching or expanding that slinky energy and encouraging it to open for better energy flow and greater mobility. So, you can now relate to how the analogy of the slinky fits perfectly into stretching your body. Get ready to stretch the excess energy and feel it leave your body as you open yourself up to do so.

7. Enjoy a Massage or Reiki: Another thing you can do to balance the energy within your body is get a relaxing massage or a reiki session to balance your energy systems. Remember that slinky we talked about? In my private practice, I have worked on individuals who have literally gained an inch or two in height after just one to four sessions. As I have released the muscular restrictions or blocked energy within their body, their internal slinky has expanded, leaving them feeling lighter and freer. It's amazing how our bodies can expand when we allow the tension to be released. Reiki alone can also create greater energy flow, relaxing the body and calming the nervous system.

8. Feel To Heal: Practice self-healing and balancing with Reiki energy healing daily. If you have not yet learned Heart Centered Reiki energy healing, I strongly encourage you to do so. Reiki is a natural energy healing modality that can be a part of your everyday life for greater balance, lightness, peace, and freedom. This universal life force for healing is available to everyone, and its energy supersedes culture, religion, personal belief systems, gender, or anything that might seek to divide one from the presence of divine. There is something beautiful that happens when we practice self-care on a consistent basis through Heart Centered Reiki energy healing. As you learn to communicate and integrate the physical sensations showing up in your body, it will bring greater balance between your mind, body, and spirit. You will also have a wonderful sense of accomplishment when you do so. With that increased knowledge, you can then offer Heart Centered Reiki to others. Perhaps there is a Reiki Master in you just waiting to be discovered. If you are an existing Reiki Master, I would encourage continued healing and self-care daily. As a Heart Centered Reiki Master Teacher, I have personally seen countless individuals all over the world find deeper healing for themselves. To

learn more about Heart Centered Reiki energy healing and its benefits you can visit *heartcenteredreiki.org* to enroll.

9. Get Grounded: One of the most beneficial things that you can do to transmute this excess energy coursing through your body is to ground your body daily. Place your bare feet on the earth or in a stream for at least ten minutes. The benefits of grounding are numerous. If you've never heard of grounding, you can think of it this way. You are an intricate being of light frequencies created in bioelectrical form, living on an electrical planet. Wouldn't it make sense to plug into the frequencies for a naturally balanced charge? Your heart, muscles, immune system, nervous system, brain, cells, and every aspect of you transmits multiple frequencies. Keep in mind that everything and everyone around you also puts out various frequencies. Some frequencies like radio waves, electromagnetic waves, ultrasound waves, microwaves, etc. can pass through you. These frequency waves can create an energetic entanglement which can be compared to static on a television. If you'd like a clear channel within your circuitry system, connect with the earth. The negative ions and frequencies of the earth are designed to connect with your physical body, while at the same time, supporting you in releasing the positive ions in your body to restore its balance. Grounding has been shown to balance energy, induce calmness, reduce inflammation, and support your body's immune system to heal faster.

10. Forgive To Live: And finally, let's energetically release you from any buried emotion that may be trapped in your body by forgiving yourself and others. Practicing compassion, kindness, and love will benefit you greatly, as those alone hold an energy of peace. When we look at the emotional and mental aspect, repressed emotion can create feelings of anxiousness. Think of a pressure cooker, which is a special pot that seals in

the steam. The steam builds up, cooking the food. Let's face it, our bodies were never meant to be pressure cookers. Imagine all the negative repressed emotions building up steam in your own body with nowhere to go because you refuse to let go of them. Are you getting the picture? Forgiving yourself, practicing kindness, compassion, and love, invites the steam of repressed emotions to be released little by little. As you do this you will feel lighter, calmer, and freer.

"You are an infinitely beautiful being of light. You were created with a vibrational energy that has the capacity to move beyond the speed of light, magically touching hearts with your presence here. Shine brightly and unapologetically with you whole heart, mind, and soul."

- Leslie Paramore

Chapter 19

Indicator 2 - Erratic Sleep Patterns

Let's talk about what we feel many individuals are experiencing in today's world - lack of sleep. Many individuals are struggling with not being able to sleep or are having sleep disturbances or disruptions. There can be many medical indicators that can contribute to lack of sleep, however, for the purposes of this material, if all medical situations have been ruled out, we can look to other indicators pointing toward ascension.

I believe that most of our society is sleep deprived and have placed their bodies on auto pilot to get through the demands of the day. Billions of dollars are spent on products that will boost our energy levels to offer some relief from fatigue or at least make it more manageable. These quick fixes are what I refer to as the band aide fix. It covers up the issue however, consuming coffee or energy drinks really doesn't fix anything. We trick our bodies into going high until we hit the low with nowhere to go but to bed, yet somehow, we just can't seem to sleep.

In terms of addressing ascension, lack of sleep can be due to having excess vibrational energy moving through your energy systems, the chakras, or meridians, which are energy lines connected to the body's organ systems. Remember that buzzing sensation we talked about earlier. Your circuitry systems are lighting up and the timing isn't always convenient. As mentioned earlier in this material, erratic sleep disturbances were a particularly difficult one for me a few years ago. When I laid down to go to sleep, my body would begin shaking uncontrollably which made sleep virtually impossible.

Keep in mind, reasons for lack of sleep are not necessarily this severe for everyone. You may simply have difficulty shutting down. Know that the earth's vibrational shifts will work with you according to what you can process or assimilate vibrationally. It can vary from night to night what that might look like for you. Sometimes this means less sleep, no sleep, or what I humorously call, adequate sleep.

No matter what you may be experiencing at this time, remember to honor your body through this temporary process. Yes, I said temporary. Let that statement be the light at the end of your tunnel. Often the ascension indicators are temporary. As we move through the energy shifts, we become adapted to them.

Allow me to give you a quick personal reference for adaptation. When I was in my twenties, I was tired all the time. I woke up tired, I functioned through the day tired, and I went to bed tired. I honestly thought everyone was like that; like it was part of a debilitating human condition, and it was my full-time job to live with it. I was conditioned to have ten to twelve hours of sleep, yet even then, I never felt rested. Fast forward a few years later, I now require very little sleep. I have been known to have as little as three to four hours of sleep and have the ability to function completely fine the next day. I feel alive and energized.

What do you think happened? If you said, "You experienced a vibrational shift, you are correct." Now keep in mind, this vibrational shift did not happen overnight. It took years to occur. As I awakened spiritually, I began to require less sleep. Look at it this way, it's better to have four solid hours of sleep, then eight hours of tossing and turning.

From what I have come to understand through channeling divine presence, as we shift toward ascension, our bodies will require less and less sleep. If you are one who loves to sleep, you may find that over a period of undisclosed time you may become more like me. You'll see sleep as a waste of your precious time here. When I was in my twenties, I used to love going to bed and I dreaded getting up. Today I find myself getting up as early as 3:00 am to greet a new day of creative possibilities. The higher the vibration, the less physical needs such as sleep, you will require. Now I love rising to greatness every new day and making the most of it and you can too.

As a side note, you've got to learn how to navigate your way through such things as lack of sleep, by thinking outside the box. As you move through this transitional period, I have provided some suggestions in the next chapter that you can integrate into your life to create calmer rest periods as you engage in calming activities prior to rest. Hopefully, the suggestions provided, as well as further insights, will offer the support that you need to create a vibrate life worth living.

Chapter 20

Balancing Erratic Sleep Patterns

Let's face it, there is nothing better than a restful sleep where our mind, body and spirit gets to shut down from all the cares and concerns of the world. A good nights sleep recharges our internal battery systems, preparing us for the starting line of the next day. As one who has typically been a light sleeper, I personally, have found the following suggestions extremely helpful.

1. Ground Your Energy: If it is possible, and as mentioned before, go out and ground with the earth. This alone can be very calming to the nervous system, inviting the balance of negative ions to enter your body, freeing up the erratic energy within you. Nighttime grounding is especially supportive when you take the time to do so as it supports the natural circadian rhythms of your body in parallel to the day and night cycles of the earth. Sunset is the perfect time to ground yourself into a better night's sleep.

2. Relax in Epsom Salts: Immerse yourself in a hot lavender bath of Epsom salts for at least fifteen to twenty minutes about a half hour before you are ready to retire for the night. The lavender scents will naturally induce subtle mental relax-

ation, while the natural Epson Salts will decrease any muscle tension being held within your body. When Epsom salt is dissolved into the water it releases magnesium and sulfate ions which are then absorbed into the skin. Magnesium helps your brain to produce neurotransmitters that induce sleep and reduce stress. About 2 cups of Epsom salts in a hot bath, will get you to where you're going . . . a better night's sleep.

3. Surround Yourself With Soothing Sounds: Gentle sounds can be very soothing to the soul. To place yourself in a relaxed state, you can listen to soft music that is specifically designed to induce relaxation, peace, and comfort. There are many choices for beautiful instrumental music on You Tube, or perhaps there's a relaxing CD that you have that hasn't been played in a while. Using the vibration of sound can ultimately carry you away note by note as you drift into a restful sleep. Make this a part of your nightly routine so that your body can energetically attune to relaxing music. Consistency is key.

4. Be Guided To Sleep: As another alternative, you can also listen to guided meditations specifically created for sleep. These typically have soft music coupled with words to induce sleep by taking you on a visual journey away from the cares of the world. As one who has written, recorded, and produced guided meditations, they most certainly have the ability to lull you into a gentle space of relaxation and peace. Keep in mind that the energy transferred during the guided meditations will work with you on multiple levels, inducing deep relaxation physically, emotionally, mentally, and spiritually.

5. Drink Comfort Teas: Drink herbal teas or warm liquids that are specifically designed for calming or for sleep. Some suggestions would be chamomile tea, or sleepy time teas. You can go to most grocery stores or health food stores to start

implementing a nice cup of tea about a half hour before bed. As an extra step, you can visualize the warm liquids washing all tension out of your body, soothing it for a relaxing night's sleep.

6. Embrace The Experience: Do not resist your experience. Embrace it. When we resist an experience, it only creates more resistance within our bodies. If you happen to wake up in the evening, do your best to embrace it and breathe deeply, allowing the energy to move through you with your breath. Draw your breath deeply into your diaphragm and then release it. This will support further relaxation. Focusing on your breath moving in and out of your body can be very soothing and relaxing.

7. Listen For Insights: Give your experience meaning by leaving a pen and pad by your bedside to jot down insights, inspiration, or spiritual impressions that may come through in those wee hours where you find yourself laying there. Often the best messages for the soul come through openness of heart and stillness. When I went through 8 months of shaking through my body, I often would put the night to good use, opening my heart up to messages that were waiting to come through. You might be surprised at what comes through during the perfect time for you.

8. Let Go of Expectations: Be in the right mindset and heart set by visualizing yourself resting comfortably, giving yourself permission to do so. Our expectations can sometimes overrule experiencing a good night's sleep. If we expect we will not sleep, it will often be manifested and created merely by our thoughts. Imagine what it would be like allowing your thoughts to rest and inviting that energy to filter through to the rest of your body.

9. Use Support Systems: Use a weighted blanket for grounding or security. This can help calm the body into feeling safe and secure. To support grounding you as you sleep, you can also use an alternative like a rice bag warmed up for comfort. When I struggled with sleep or keeping my body calm, I would often lay an oval rock that had some weight to it, on my solar plexus chakra which would have a calming effect on my body.\

10. Turn Of The Lights: Refrain from engaging in cell phone activity or computer activity just prior to sleep. The light from those bright screens can often interfere with your sleep as they can confuse the sleep chemicals of the body into thinking it daytime. Specialized cells in the retinas of your eyes process light and tell the brain whether it is day or night and can advance or delay our sleep-wake cycles. Exposure to light can make it difficult to fall asleep and return to sleep when awakened. Save screen time for the day and sleep time for night. I hope you will find these suggestions helpful as you find yourself drifting into a peaceful night's sleep.

Chapter 21

Indicator 3 - Changes in Diet Preferences

It may seem that lately, your relationship with food has gone belly up, or at least that's how it may appear. In shifting your vibrational reality, you may suddenly find that foods that you used to like no longer agree with your digestive system or your palette. As mentioned earlier, these changes may not be evident in everyone and this shift may occur suddenly or gradually. Much of our experiences are based on our own internal belief systems about food and our relationship to it.

In your ascension process your body is literally raising in vibration, so therefore it may call for foods that are living with energy instead of the low energy of other worldly foods. You may feel the need to steer away from eating processed foods, as your body may be craving live enzymes and nutrients to energetically support you. Aside from your physical body, remember you have a total of four bodies to consider; your physical body, your emotional body, your spiritual body, and your mental body, which are all connected to some degree yet, may be vibrating at different frequencies. How can you be one vibrational being if all four of your bodies are vibrating at various frequencies?

The truth is each of us must feed our bodies according to what they are energetically craving. Let's first look at your emotions. Emotionally you may crave more intimacy and connection with yourself. Next, let's look at your mental state. Mentally, you may wish to feed your mind with things that nourish it intellectually, like a good book. Of course, we can't forget about the spiritual aspect of you. Spiritually, you may wish to absorb the beautiful energies of calming meditation or yoga. And finally, physically, you may start craving high vibrational foods such as salads, smoothies, raw nuts, fruits, or vegetables. Some simple examples of how you might choose to nourish each body. Be sure to intuitively listen to what your four bodies require as you honor yourself through this process. This is where your intuition comes in. Ask your body what it needs.

There have been times that I have had impressions to purchase certain foods without knowing why, yet I have learned to listen to those intuitive hunches. What is interesting is that after I act upon the intuitive hunch and purchase the food, I later find out some of the great nutritional benefits of that particular food. For example, once I was in a health food store and felt like my body needed pure, raw cherry juice. Now, keep in mind that I had never in my life purchased such a thing, so it was quite strange that all of a sudden, I felt this nudge to get it. Later that day I found out that cherry juice has high levels of iron in it. I could share countless other experiences where I was led to consume something that I wouldn't typically eat.

Our suggestion to you is to ask your body what foods would fuel it on a daily basis. Remember, the more you listen and follow through with those gentle nudges, the more you will be tuned into your body.

Chapter 22

Balancing Changes
in Your Diet

Diet changes can be an exciting new adventure to try out new foods and to delve deeper into the intelligence of your physical body. Be aware that as you feel better physically, it will most definitely affect how you feel emotionally, mentally, and spiritually. Remember. your four bodies are digesting the energies of life simultaneously. Here are some suggestions to support your brand new diet shift.

1. Ask Questions: Ask your body what it wants to eat and then listen for the answer. If you could eat a high vibrational food that would resonate and integrate perfectly with your body, what would that be? You might be surprised at how your body will let you know through some subtle intuitive impressions. I'd like to extend a little caution here. Don't be fooled by false impressions that could keep your body out of alignment. Once as I was going through diet changes, I found myself craving lemon meringue pie, however, that doesn't mean I went out and bought one. With this sugar craving, I asked my body, "What is it that you really need at this time?" and I heard, "Lemons – Your body wants to cleanse." So simply put, don't cave to the cravings that are not the best and highest good for your body.

2. Feel for The Feedback: One of the best ways to test whether your body wants a particular food is to feel the food. After eating a certain food, how does your body feel? Does it feel calm inside or are you bloated and in pain? Your body speaks, so learn to listen to the feedback it offers you. Your body really does want to be your best friend; however, you must meet it in the middle with adjustments that will benefit your mind, body, and spirit. Remember, feel for the feedback.

3. Consult an Expert: If you are unsure about what foods could best serve your body, there are many food experts that can support you in assimilating physical change within your body. Perhaps you have an unknown allergy to a food substance you've been eating for years, and this could be the cause of your discomfort. Learn what can work for you by exploring possibilities for greater health that will support your physical body. As you do, your mind will become clearer, and your ability to tune into your intuition will increase.

4. Exercise Your Body: Movement is encouraged for greater digestion to support the absorption and assimilation of the foods that you eat. Movement of your body moves energy and that includes your food. One of the forms of exercise that I love to do is jumping on a mini trampoline. This is a wonderful way to move the digestion of food and it also supports oxygenation of the blood and lymphatic drainage. If we eat and do not move, the excess energy of food is stored as excess fat, which in turn creates energy blockages, which in turn creates dis-ease within the body. You've got to move it to lose it! Now let's commit to movement.

5. Slow Down: I just talked about the movement of your body and now I'd like to talk about another kind of movement.

Slow down your eating habits and enjoy the new changes that are taking place. Take time to feel the energy of the food connecting with your body. This is an area that I admit I need to practice more. Sometimes I find myself rushing while eating, so I can move onto the next activity of my day. It's a habit that started as a child because I was always rushing through my meal to get the homemade cake that was waiting for me. Meditative eating is a good rule of thumb to adopt while eating. Feel the textures in your mouth, look at the colors, smell the aroma, and also, give gratitude for the experience. I really need to work on this one. Note to self. Slow down.

6. Water Your Vessel: Along with food, let water be your best friend by drinking adequate amounts per day. You know your body. Ask how much water it wishes to have throughout the day. If you have been exercising, it's a good idea to hydrate before, during, and after your routine. Also I might suggest taking about ½ a teaspoon of sea salt in water in the morning which can help support the absorption of water as it permeates through the cell walls.

7. Be Grateful: One of the most important shifts you can make as you take food into your body is to be grateful. Eating food with the energy of gratitude raises the frequency of the food and also your experience. Receive all food with gratitude and love. See any possible physical impurities, transforming into the highest vibrational food that will bless your body, your mind, and your spirit.

Chapter 23

Indicator 4 - Changes in Lifestyle

Let's face it, there are many different kinds of lifestyles and that's what makes life rather interesting. At one time you may have been the type of person that loved to be in the limelight and around large crowds, however, now you may suddenly find yourself seeking seclusion or alone time. This may have caught you off guard or has been a gradual shift in your personal lifestyle. Let me place your mind and heart at ease.

This new lifestyle change is all part of creating a new energetic space for yourself to discover the new you. You are now removing yourself from old experiences, situations, or individuals that no longer resonate with your high vibe.

Here's a simple analogy to visualize. When a caterpillar is building its cocoon, it certainly doesn't invite the neighborhood caterpillars to join it as it retreats to solitude for inner transformation. Although a silly analogy, it holds true for exactly what may be occurring for you in this very moment. Imagine a caterpillar trying desperately to build its cocoon as other caterpillars nudge their way through, invading the space of creation for inner and outer change. The energetic entanglement would sabotage the whole effort and the caterpillar would more than likely die. You see, there is an instinctual act that the caterpillar knows it must do alone, void of any other thing in order to rise to its greatest expression of creation and that instinct is also within you.

Much like a butterfly seeks silent refuge and transformation within the walls of a cocoon, you are doing the same, so be sure to honor yourself and your quiet time. Creating time to be alone will support you in being in a space where you can more easily connect with stillness and therefore the sound of spirit speaking to you. It is okay to move away from the hustle and bustle of life and take time for yourself. This creates time for listening, contemplating, reflection, and relaxation, as you create new ways of engaging with your beautifully new life experiences.

Your old life is fading away and you now have the opportunity to fill up the spaces within yourself that you may have somehow forgotten or left behind. As a side note, if others in your life express concern about your change in behavior, you can say you are taking time to reevaluate your life to figure out what's working or not working for you. Reassure the onlookers that your change in lifestyle has nothing to do with them and to not take it personally. A true friend will respect your wishes and offer you the support and space that you need as you transform your life into new ways of thinking and being. Other friends may fall away and in that case it's your opportunity to let them go on their way to their new life trusting that all is working out for the greater good of everyone concerned. Trust in the process designed to create the best life for you.

Chapter 24

Balancing Changes in Lifestyle

With your new lifestyle, sometimes putting the pieces all together can feel a little bit overwhelming, so here are some creative suggestions that can support you through the process of navigating what your new life will look like right now.

1. Be Alone: Give yourself permission every day to be alone with no distractions or interruptions. In essence, place yourself on a timeout from the everyday goings on of life. Sit in complete stillness for at least twenty minutes while focusing on calm energy moving through your body with every conscious breath. Ask yourself, "Who are you in this silence?" Then listen for the answer. If you don't hear anything, be patient. See yourself as an empty book just waiting to be written. The words will come and when they do, I am sure you will write a best seller for your life.

2. Consider Journaling: You might be surprised to learn that writing and English were not exactly my favorite subjects in school, yet I somehow became an author. If this is possible for me, then imagine the unlimited possibilities for you. Begin journaling by writing down what ways you would like to simplify your life. An idea could be something like spending more

time in nature, more time with a good book, or more time moving your body for greater energy flow. You know yourself better than anyone as you write your thoughts down. After writing some ideas down, be sure to act and implement the ideas gradually as it is comfortable to you. You might implement one new idea each day for a week to integrate it into your new way of life.

3. Create Your Vision: A great place to start creating your vision is by creating a vision board. A vision board is simply a collage of pictures, words, symbols, or affirmative statements that represent your goals and dreams for your new life. It is a visual representation to inspire you as a daily reminder of what is important to you. To get an idea of what to place on your vision board, you can start by exploring what you value in life. What really matters to you? What makes your heart sing? What do you feel passionate about? What motivates you to claim your dreams? Who are you in your most creative expression of you? Fill the vision board with pictures, words, symbols, positive statements, or anything that will inspire you on a daily basis. As a side note to this, there is a common misconception that a vision board will magically make your dream materialize however, there is more to it than that. To experience your dreams, you must first create your dreams. Start by energetically connecting with your vision board daily, allowing yourself to feel the emotion of it. Feel the emotion behind seeing yourself already having created your new lifestyle. And finally, move into action and goal setting to create it. Before you know it, you will be surrounded by it, living the dreams you once created on your vision board.

4. Celebrate You: Take time for celebration. I have a saying, *"Every day is a birthday; a day to celebrate the brand new you."* Create a me day, a day where you celebrate time alone with you

to do whatever your heart leads you to do. I started initiating "Me Days" a few years ago within my own life and it is the perfect recharge that can offer fresh perspective and energy for the next best thing evolving in your life. This kind of day helps you to get comfortable with spending time with you and will give you a positive lift of energy and time to breathe as you move into your newfound life. I love, "Me Days." They always leave me feeling so appreciative of my time with others and of course, also myself.

5. Be Open to Change: Now that your old life is moving away from you, open your heart up to change and newfound possibilities. A wonderful mantra associated with this change could be, *"I now open my heart to the infinite possibilities all around me."* Imagine your heart as a flower opening to a fresh new rain and imagine each of those raindrops nourishing you with the infinite possibilities of your life. Imagine how you would blossom with a heart open to change. Your lifestyle is changing and that is okay. Give yourself permission to move with change, creating a lifestyle that resonates with who you are becoming.

Chapter 25

Indicator 5 - Displacement or Upheaval

Let's face it, life can be filled with twists and turns and the unexpected, and at times it can feel like a roller coaster ride of experiences mixed with a variety of emotions. Individuals for the most part, like the familiar. They get comfortable with structure, routine, and predictability, so when the unexpected occurs, it can feel challenging and at times, indescribably overwhelming. In the energy shifts connected with ascension, many individuals find themselves uprooted from their normal lives as they shift toward higher ways of thinking, being and becoming the highest version of themselves.

Perhaps during this time, you have a feeling that some great change is looming on the horizon, or perhaps you are in the middle of what may feel like a huge earthquake in your life. Despite these uncomfortable feelings it can serve you to trust in the displacement or upheaval that you may be experiencing right now. The types of shifts that we are referring to are huge life changes. Often great shifts occur in the form of the loss of a job, moving to a new area, or a significant change in your current relationships with marriage, friends, coworkers, or family. When we allow the mind to view the physical aspect of this, it can be rather unsettling because humans tend to cling to the familiar and often resist sudden change. Take a deep breath . . . and trust that your higher self knows its purpose and that you are exactly where you need to be.

As a simple analogy, visualize for a moment a plant who has outgrown the pot it was initially planted in. Its roots have filled the pot, and the soil has been depleted of essential nutrients. To remain there would be to stunt the growth of the plant and its fullest potential to bloom. Once repotted, it takes some time for the plant to acclimatize to its new surroundings. It needs to connect with the new soil and extend and strengthen its roots. Displacement may be the initial sensation, yet, with further exploration, the plant has literally been placed in a wonderful opportunity to thrive in its new surroundings.

In my life I have been uprooted many times by conscious choice. I have constantly evaluated and reevaluated what is working and not working in my life. It hasn't been easy. In fact, consciously choosing to uproot for growth can be incredibly challenging, yet, totally worth the results. Sometimes it may feel that someone made the choice for you, like when someone ends a relationship, while other times you may consciously decide on your own to leave a job that feels stale. No matter what the circumstance, whether it seems like you have chosen it or not chosen it, what matters is how you choose to meet it. The energy of displacement or upheaval indicates that you have outgrown your space. It's time to move forward, inviting new energy for growth and inner discovery. It's time to bloom.

Chapter 26

Balancing Displacement or Upheaval

Although feeling of displacement or upheaval can be unsettling, it requires on to let go on deeper levels. Trust plays a key factor in how well one can adapt to the changes. Some things that you can do to support yourself through any feelings of displacement or upheaval are the following:

1. Be Open to Possibilities: As mentioned, feelings of displacement can be unsettling, however, I would like you to consider something that may expand your view of this situation. Many people in life have found themselves limited by jobs or relationships that they really do not enjoy. They settle in, and grin and bear it. Perhaps you've been there or are there right now. Without warning, life becomes a maze of walls, restrictions, limitations, and dead ends, yet most everyone simply goes along with it, until the unexpected occurs. Some life disruption interferes, and the individual finds themselves in a temporary period of displacement. The mind struggles with it because it feels uncomfortable, and its instinct is to resist the unknown and cleave to what once was, yet perhaps there's an-

other perspective that we'd wish you to consider about this thing called, displacement.

Imagine the Universe saying, *"Your lesson here is done. You no longer have to be trapped in the maze of limitation."* Imagine the walls being lifted from the maze of your mind, exposing the truth. Imagine yourself being surrounded by 360 degrees of possibilities and how expansive that would feel to you if nothing were getting in your way. You are free to create your unlimited life. You have passed an initiation of sorts and the Universe is applauding you all the way. In reality, displacement is a gift to you, opening up to the freedom to create the new life now before you.

2. Trust Deeper: If something falls way like the loss of a job, trust that you have simply outgrown it and your soul is calling you to step into new positions that resonate with your soul's next step. Sit with the situation and ask yourself, *"Now what? What is my soul's next step?" If your soul could choose a path what would that be in absolutely nothing was in your way? Where would that lead you? And how would it feel to walk on that path?"* Trust deeper in knowing that everything conspires to happen for you as you lean into your new life.

3. Step Out of Resistance: It is extremely helpful to move into an awareness of acceptance. Clinging to what was just creates more resistance within your life and can block what is wanting to come through for you. Instead of resisting the idea of upheaval, focus on what you would like to see yourself moving into from right where you are. As you see yourself moving forward, your intended focus is what creates your experiences. If you focus on being uprooted, you will continue to feel that way until you move into acceptance. Imagine a magnifying glass focusing on the expansion of your soul. What would ma-

terialize before your eyes? What tiny details would come into view for the new deeply rooted you who is now ready to accept the best possible outcomes.

4. Observe and Acknowledge Your Feelings: One of the best ways to move through displacement is by simply observing the feeling without judgment. See yourself at the starting point of your life as you find new ways to reconnect with you. Often feelings of being displaced are in relation to being out of alignment within ourselves. Sometimes we can lose ourselves in life's experiences, leaving ourselves with feelings of being completely lost. If it seems that you have lost yourself, the good news is you can once again find yourself by simply observing where you are right now.

5. Get Creative: Ground yourself in something that feels satisfying and fulfilling to you. It might be something simple like working with clay or painting a picture or singing. This creative energy will support you at the starting point of your new life. The art of expression comes from your sacral chakra which can then move into your root chakra grounding you in something you love. As you build upon the energy, it can open doorways to new possibilities for your life. The things that you enjoy doing right now can be clues to where your new life is waiting. Explore the creative side of you for the absolute best clues designed just for you.

6. Visualization Exercises: If you could imagine creating the absolute best life for yourself, what would that look like? Using visualization techniques to support yourself through feelings of displacement can be helpful. It is a simple as using your vivid imagination where possibilities are endless. Visualization is kind of like creating a mental vision board that is in motion and filled with lots of energy information. In your visualiza-

tion, see yourself walking along a path that leads to your new life. What do you see as you walk along it? Where are you going? Where do you live? What kind of job do you see yourself enjoying? Who are your friends? What brings you joy? This is a wonderful way to awaken the spiritual part of yourself to show you the way and ground you in what is already within your energy field. Play with it and have fun. No dream is too big if you can imagine it. Remember displacement is a gift. It gives you 360 degrees of choices all around you. Now, where do you see yourself going?

"There is nothing more courageous than when a human heart opens itself up to vulnerability without any thought of how it will be perceived. It opens unapologetically, perfectly raw, and real, while roaring openly at the dark night, calling in its grand awakening."

-Leslie Paramore

Chapter 27

Indicator 6 - Letting Go of Outcomes

You will know that you are making great spiritual strides in your awakening process when you find yourself letting go or detaching from any outcomes in your personal life or anything that is surrounding your life. This is a process that some may know as, letting go.

Often times in life individuals tend to try and control everything around them, and quite frankly, it can be rather exhausting long term. In the past, you may have found yourself trying to appease others to receive greater acceptance, or you may have played the role of referee between people to create peace, or you may have stepped in to fix other people's situations to prevent emotional warfare. Life became one drama after another, where you may have put out more than your share of fires.

As you awaken to greater consciousness, you begin to see life differently. You begin to see the perfection within the imperfection of each and every experience. You begin to see the value and wisdom offered to every individual as they learn to problem solve and navigate their way around the challenges that life often presents. You step back as the silent observer, trusting that all experiences are designed to teach some valuable life lesson or spiritual awareness. You are calm, centered, and confident, knowing that all is working together for the highest good of all.

At first glance, from the onlookers, they may be confused by your calm demeanor, neutral position, or refusal to get in the middle of issues that belong to others. Others may even become upset with you, yet, when you learn to detach from the outcomes, you willingly receive the accusations with a position of nonjudgement. It may initially appear to others that you've turned your internal heart switch to the uncaring position. You are no longer reacting to external stimuli that used to trigger you into strong emotional reactions such as fear, anger, or worry. Your new look can be confusing to the onlookers, yet I urge you to hold your ground, meaning ground your heart in trusting that all is working out for the greater good of all as you center yourself in a reassuring trust.

With this shift, you are now learning to trust on deeper levels by seeing past the illusion of what may be showing up on the physical level. Letting go of outcomes simply means that you are learning to trust in the unseen, knowing that everything, both negative and positive, are working out for the greater good of all concerned. You are becoming more confident as you step into spiritual mastery. You see all outcomes unfolding as they should be, no longer taking the position of judge and ruler over other people's lives.

Keep in mind that this shift takes practice. You may at times find yourself slipping back into old habits, however, the important thing is that you self-correct and move on. In time, you will simply move more and more into acceptance, trusting that the Universe is supporting the inner workings of all souls. In essence, letting go is letting the Spirit of the God within you move through your life in miraculous ways, to greater heights of consciousness. Imagine shedding the limitations of being human and stepping into a more conscious and expanded way of being and how that would not only bring you to new heights, but others as well, just by letting go of out-comes.

"There is no such thing as opposition. Only mountains of beautiful opportunities within the walls of your own soul."

Leslie Paramore

Chapter 28

Balancing Letting Go of Outcomes

The art of letting go can be challenging, however, as you allow trust and gratitude to guide your steps you will find it easier and easier to step into pure acceptance for what is. You will ultimately see the perfection within the imperfection of this physical world and witness the beauty all around you, releasing your heart to peace. Some suggestions that you can implement to support yourself in this shift now occurring, are the following:

1. Practice Being the Master: It takes practice to let go and at times you may find yourself getting attached to an outcome or trying to magically will your supernatural powers over a situation that suddenly pops up in your life. Practice recognizing when those attachments occur and then release them like you would a balloon filled with helium. Practice trusting in all outcomes for the greater good of all, including yourself. You may find yourself feeling relieved as you allow yourself to let go of control, allowing the flow of life to move through your new-found ways of being. I promise, just like the helium balloon, you will feel lighter and freer.

2. Show Kindness and Empathy: Being detached does not mean we erase our ability to show kindness or empathy toward ourselves as a collective. You can express empathy and validate without getting attached to the outcome. This shows individuals that you care without helping to fuel the emotion they may be feeling about a particular situation. A simple empathetic statement might be, "I am so sorry for the pain you are experiencing. I just know that somehow this will work itself out." In offering such a statement you are showing empathy, which displays a caring heart. Also, be sure to extend the same love to yourself as you are met with situations that are challenging.

3. Refuse to Interfere: It's okay to allow yourself and others to experience life without trying to interfere and make things better. If you think of it, when you try to fix somebody's challenge or situation, energetically, you are robbing them of the opportunity to succeed in that area of their life. Allowing others to take accountability for their lives will do more good than anything and will expedite the awakening process for all.

4. Empower Situations: Many individuals tend to get energetically entangled in situations, meaning, they take on the negative emotion of another and then add their own emotions to it, which simply adds to the chaotic energy, thus magnifying it. For people who are struggling, instead of seeing them in victim energy, see them as the victor of that situation. See them being empowered and working through it. An empowering statement might be, "I just know in my heart you will work through this and come out shining." Offering this statement will instill confidence within the person who may be struggling with an issue.

5. Practice Observing: As mentioned earlier, placing yourself in the position of the confident observer can energetically support situations that may be occurring in your life as well as the lives of those around you. Now, with that being said, I feel it important to note that being the observer doesn't necessarily apply to situations when a person is in danger. If a child is being harmed, you will certainly not stand by and allow that to occur. Tune into the situations that present themselves and determine for yourself what warrants observation and what warrants intervention.

6. Envision All Situations Resolved: One of the ways that you can practice being the observer is seeing conflict or out of balance situations coming to a positive resolution. See all players awakening to themselves, thus inviting harmony into their lives. I suppose we could use the analogy of a dominos scenario. Visualize yourself as the first domino sending energy from you to all other dominos in your path. You are but one domino, however, as you see all things resolved, it sends a powerful energy into the lives of countless individuals. The old ways of life fall, and a new life can begin for all.

As you move through this material, you may discover other ways that you can support yourself as an observer. Be open to some of that inspiration. Remember, when a baby begins to walk, it has the occasional tumble. It is a natural progression that needs to happen in order for the baby to master walking. In essence, we are all learning to master the art of walking through life with its twists and turns, ups and downs, and unexpected bumps. It can be a roller coaster ride, yet we cannot walk for someone else. Each of us must walk step by step and become the master of our own creations both positive and negative. We can stand firm as the observer, for all cheering each of us on, knowing we will eventually become masters of ourselves and our awakening.

As time moves on your ability to let go will become easier and more freeing. As you do so, you will find that it will create an energetic ripple effect within your life. Things that no longer resonate with your energy field will naturally fade away with every passing thought of letting go. Like the natural tides of the ocean, new energy will move in and old energy will move out as the ebb and tides of life work with your soul on mysterious levels. Letting go is a spiritual practice that you will master to various levels over and over again as you invite divine love into each and every experience that you are privelidged to observe through the divine mind of God.

See yourself letting go of your old self right now. As you do, you'll be lighter, freer and happier than you've ever been.

"A true leader never seeks for followers. Instead, a true leader will lovingly direct a soul to follow the paths of light within their own divine heart."

- Leslie Paramore

Chapter 29

Indicator 7 - Changes in Belief Systems

Many individuals who are experiencing an awakening find themselves letting go of old belief systems, the traditional ways of their culture, or teachings of their family tribe. Much like a baby bird has an instinctual timetable to fly from its nest, in a similar way, some of us are being called to soar past our limiting belief systems.

For example, a quite common change in belief systems may revolve around religious beliefs. You may have been brought up in a particular religion, however, something instinctual calls you to move beyond that experience to explore other possibilities. Maybe you move from being religious to spiritual, or from spiritual to religious, or from atheist to Buddhist. As you simply view these changes as things you are choosing to experience for the growth and awareness of your soul, you really can't make a poor decision when you are thirsting for expansion. Every experience holds value, as each provides contrast and acts as a catalyst to bring you to exactly where you were destined to be.

For myself, I wasn't raised with any religion, however, I was taught to be kind, compassionate, and considerate, along with other ways to be a good member of society. With no foundational religious beliefs, I created a shift in my twenties. Something instinctually called me to expand my view and to explore religion. For a period of eight years, I studied many religions and became deeply involved in a few, however, in time, I moved into a more spiritual point of view on life, adopting the belief that everything is connected and part of grand, divine design. I like to see life as this beautiful kaleidoscope working together to create a divine design that is in the best and highest good of all. We each represent of portion of the kaleidoscope, shifting colors, designs, locations, and positions.

When you find yourself changing your belief systems, whether it be religious beliefs, spiritual beliefs, scientific beliefs, family beliefs, social beliefs, political beliefs, food beliefs, or any belief that once created a foundational structure for you to stand on, it can be unsettling. You may receive some resistance from your family, friends, coworkers, or individuals that you've acquainted yourself with through various social gatherings revolving around those former belief systems. Nonetheless, don't lose heart, you are pulling away from foundational teachings and spreading your wings into the infinite possibilities all around you.

You have now come to a point in your life where you no longer seek answers from those around of you, however, instead, choose to go deeper within yourself for all the truths that are waiting to be unveiled. This process can take a considerable amount of time, as you seek and listen to your inner voice of the I Am presence within you.

Allow us to a reassure you, you have a unique spiritual path and purpose that is unfolding. Be patient with yourself. Look forward to the unique discoveries within you. You are on the right path for awakening your divine heart.

Chapter 30

Balancing Changes in Belief Systems

Here you are questioning everything you thought you once knew. Well, did you think that everything in your life would always stay the same? Are you content to stifle your growth for the appeasement or approval of others?

You've outgrown the shoes you've been walking in and now you appear to be heading in a new direction, but you're not exactly sure where that's going. As mentioned, changes in belief systems can feel unsettling, adding to the displacement that you may already be feeling, however, hopefully this material will provide some things that will support you through the expansion that is now taking place within your life. Here are some simple suggestions that can support you in changing your belief systems.

1. Be Open to Change: The one thing that tends to keep people from changing their belief systems is the emotion of fear. This fear can come in the form of many ugly faces. Fear of rejection, fear of the unknown, fear of disapproval, fear of failure, fear of judgment, fear of loss, fear of making a mistake, fear of hurting others and the list goes on. So the question is, how can you go through change even though you may be feeling this fear that is staring you in the face?

Accept it. That's right, acknowledge that you are feeling fear, however, do not let that fear keep you from discovering what's on the other side of it. Often times you will find that, on the other side of the wall of fear, lays your infinite power.

For example, I once had a belief system that due to my fear of heights, I could not climb a particular mountain that spiraled 1500 feet into the sky. Despite this, I attempted to climb the mountain anyway. There were ten trail markers that pointed the way to the top, and I froze at marker number seven. My body was tired, weak, shaking, and dizzy. I desperately wanted to head back down to a false sense of safety. Just as I was about to do so, a woman heading down the trail from the top looked at me and said, "If I can do it. You can do it. I'm terrified of heights!" That little bit of encouragement buoyed me to the top of the mountain where I then raised my arms in victory, because I changed a belief system I had about myself. It's okay to feel fear, however, do not let it paralyze you. Move through it, to get to the other side of you; the real you.

2. Explore with Curiosity: Do you remember when you were a child, and you were curious about everything? You naturally explored your world without judging it. You absorbed every-thing around you, the sights, sounds, smells, textures, and ex-periences from little to big. Everything was begging you to grow, to learn and discover the things changing all around you. As seasons of your life changed, leaves went from vibrant green, then suddenly they turned to brilliant colors that seemed to light up the sky, then without warning they fell to the ground, exposing the underlying structure of the tree.

Life was like that as a child; carefree, curious, and somewhat careless, yet as most grow older, they succumb to life's condi-tioning, cleaving to the familiar and acceptable, stifling out the way we once viewed the world.

The good news is, as you change limiting belief systems, you are once again invited to view the world from a child's perspective, starting a new foundation that you get to build with your conscious choices.

3. Embrace the Change: When you consciously take the position of embracing the changes taking place within you, you naturally open a flow of energy that supports that change. You are going with the flow, enjoying the journey, and discovering the parts of you that are evolving at an accelerated rate. It's what I call, "The Holy Flow." The Holy Flow occurs when universal elements of the Divine, both seen and unseen, strategically co-conspire to lead you to exactly where you are meant to be at any given moment in time. To be in such a glorious space, is like opening up the sails of your heart, inviting the breath of God to fill your sails with the divine energy it takes to bring you to the highest possible potential of your soul.

4. Release Expectations: As you release old belief systems, it's also important to release the expectations tied to yourself. Your tribal foundation is rooted within the people that have surrounded your life, yet you can't leave an island of belief systems and expect to take everyone with you. Some of your belief systems revolving around life have been like an island, keeping you limited. It's important to note that not everyone will embrace your new lifestyle changes. Some may choose to stay on the island of old beliefs, and you've got to be okay with that even if they are not okay with you leaving. Release all expectations of possible reactions of resistance from anyone affected by your changes in beliefs.

5. Navigate Consciously: If you're going to leave your old island of beliefs, you must know how to navigate the direction of your life. Allowing the tides and winds of life to toss you around from here to there with no clear intention or direction

will end up costing you precious time. You have the opportunity to set conscious intentions and navigate your heart
accordingly. Connect with what you may know as higher consciousness, God, Source, Creation, or anything that represents
divine love and step into a co-creative effort, inviting inspiration to lead you to your next step. Remember too, the whole
purpose of your life not about the destination. It's about the
details woven within your heart as you experience what life is
teaching you. Ultimately, you will know that your compass is
set on course as you begin to experience life through the eyes
of love, compassion, forgiveness and understanding.

*"You are the ripple effect. You are the stone casting yourself
into the waters of life, creating frequency waves of love or fear.
Choose wisely, for a perfect love cast out all fear."*

- Leslie Paramore

Chapter 31

Indicator 8 - Deeper Growth and Learning

As you awaken to the higher consciousness of the God within you, you will begin to exhibit deep desires for positive growth and learning. In this gradual shift, you are becoming like a conscious sponge, absorbing as much information as you can through the various sources that sudden synchronicity has to offer you.

The fact that you are engaged in this material provided to support you, is a sure sign that you are moving toward becoming an avid learner and seeker of knowledge for the purpose of your soul's path. The traditional ways of earth schooling have gone by the wayside, and you are now seeking spiritual truths designed to point the way to the truth of divine love in its fullness. Through this deeper growth and learning, you are moving beyond what was once familiar, now daring to stretch beyond the boundaries of human teachings and philosophies. You are no longer content with traditional teachings of mankind and seek to explore the unknown corridors of your soul, which holds the ultimate truth of your eternal divinity and birthright.

Due to this shift in consciousness, you may seek further enlightenment and knowledge by taking classes on spirituality, learning about deeper ways of healing, reading inspiring material, and overall seeking things that will expand the wisdom within your divine heart. Trust that you will be led accordingly and that every possible energy block of conditioning will be removed from your consciousness, starting with the root chakra, and replaced with greater and greater light and knowledge through each subsequent chakra. As a result, we are always given opportunities to learn and grow on a soul level.

We are multidimensional beings having human experience in which through the ascension process, we will ultimately obtain the power to raise even the human condition to its ultimate, glorified state.

One final note. As you seek to learn, discern wisely with your divine mind and heart connecting to higher consciousness. There is so much material in the world wide web that certain teachings will often induce conflict or contradict one another. When you are first learning to open to new ways of being and believing, it can be challenging to discern truth.

I personally have found that when I listen to the inspiration that flows to me, there will ultimately be a second witness to confirm what has been channeled through me. It will come through the words of another, or unexpected source to confirm the spiritual truth of one. And what is the spiritual truth of one? The spiritual truth of one is the only thing that expands upon itself over and over again, connecting all things and bringing a remembrance of love to us all. If what you are learning doesn't point to the ultimate source of divine love, you may want to consider changing direction. In the meantime, I urge you to keep seeking. Trust in the way that your intuition is leading you and teaching you.

Chapter 32

Balancing Deeper Growth and Learning

As you move deeper into learning about your spiritual purpose here you will want to balance your growth and learning. It is after all, a learning curve to do so, which will take some adjustments on your part. We highly suggest you go with the flow if your heart and open it up to the possibilities of learn and remembering the true essence of your soul. Some things that can support yourself in your life's growth curve are the following suggestions:

1. Learn to Discern: What you are learning can support you in going deeper within the mysteries of yourself and the path of your soul. When one is first on the spiritual path there may be a tendency to google everything under the sun to absorb as much information as possible. The problem is, humans are human, and have a sea of ideas when it comes to ascending to higher consciousness. The question is, how can you discern what material is relevant to you?

Let's use a simple analogy to go deeper with this. We can compare this situation to how you feel when you eat certain foods. If you eat an abundance of sugar, it may leave you feeling wired or somewhat ill, whereas, if you eat a beautifully made salad, it may sit better on your stomach, with a light and nourishing feeling.

Likewise, just like food, when we read material, we are energetically digesting the material consumed by our thoughts. During your digestion of such material, learn to tune into how you intuitively feel as you read various material. Some of the ways you can tune in to see how it is sitting with you is by asking some questions to measure if it resonates with your inner knowing. Do you feel calm inside? Does it make sense? Does it feel balanced? Is it easy to digest? Can you apply it to expand your life in powerful ways? Does it bring you closer to a higher power which reflects back a remembrance of your true self? A good rule of thumb to use when all is said and done is take what resonates with you and apply it to your life. Whatever brings in confusion, place it aside and move on.

2. Apply the Knowledge: Knowledge is only knowledge until you are able to integrate it into your life. A simple analogy to reference this is, if you are looking for better ways of eating to bring greater balance into your life, the first step is to research what foods could possibly work for you. Once you find what you are looking for, the next step is to create the recipes and try them out. After you try the new ways of eating, you are going to feel for feedback to see if the food is in energetic resonance with your body.

Let's apply this to the newfound spiritual wisdom you are now obtaining on your unique path. What good would it be to simply read a library of books with no application of the principles within your life. For instance, to simply read about meditation, will not benefit you unless you are willing to apply its practice. The simple practice of meditation is like testing to see if this is something that could benefit you on your path. The art of meditation is a beautiful practice, however, may not necessarily be something that will support your soul's path. Perhaps in a past life, you were a meditation guru and you have already mastered that skill. Perhaps your next step might be channeling meditations for others. Do you see how tuning in and applying the things you are learning can be beneficial in discerning whether or not it is something that will support you in knowing yourself on deeper levels? The integration and application of knowledge is the fuel to support your remembering process.

3. Be Open to Guidance: One of the most helpful things I have applied in my life to lead my soul according to the best and highest good is to leave myself open to inner guidance. One would never think to take a trip in life without first obtaining some type of guidance system like a map or GPS. Learning to be open to your internal mapping system can be helpful in ensuring a journey that will not take you away with unexpected detours or dead ends. There is an energy highway connected to a universal source which is connected to you. Tuning into a clear channel will support you in receiving the guidance that you need. Don't be afraid to ask to be led to what you are seeking internally. The Universal realms are listening to you and are fully equipped to guide you accordingly.

Let's face it, if you go to a gas station and ask for directions to California, the person is not going to give you directions to Florida. The powers that be are no different. When you ask for specific guidance, expect to receive it through some synchronistic means. The more you open yourself up to the guidance, the more you will receive. It's an exercise of trust and implementation of the guidance given. Again, always check for the feeling or impression that settles into your heart. If it feels unsettling, or you find yourself confused, you may want to wait until the message becomes so clear that you have no doubt in the direction you need to go.

"The time will come where you will cease to chase the path of learning as you invite your heart to awaken to divine, Godly truth within. Remember, in your avid learning, you are merely remembering the love that you already are."

- Leslie Paramore

Chapter 33

Indicator 9 - Changes in Reactions

Human behaviors can sometimes be predictable, based on past reactions to various circumstances. People tend to get drawn into the energies of joy, anger, frustration, or the overall energy being manifested at any given moment. People are emotional beings. It's natural to feel emotion, yet, as we awaken to our true selves, the emotion that tends to surface more and more is the emotion of divine love, which is truly an indicator that your consciousness is shifting to higher ways of thinking, being, and believing. Your once typical reactions tend to fall away, replacing them with compassion, understanding, empathy and an indescribable love for mankind, no matter what their behavior is displaying. It's a rather curious shift that can occur as the heart awakens to its source of power which is infinite and divine to the core.

Overtime, as you move into greater spiritual awareness, you may be surprised to discover that things that once caused you great upset, no longer have that particular effect on you. You are now moving into a spiritual maturity where you understand that you ultimately get to choose your emotions and your reactions regarding your personal experiences and also the external experiences surrounding you that may involve other people.

During this process of awakening, external circumstances or situations may play tricks on your mind and add a little bit of confusion as you let go of old ways of reacting. For instance, at one time you may have found that you got caught up in the tumbleweed of other people's emotions if a situation erupted in anger. In the past, you may have been drawn into and engulfed in that anger, however, now you may find yourself somehow being the calm force in any chaotic energy that finds its way around you.

A great analogy to demonstrate the energy of strength and position that you are currently experiencing can be realized by using the analogy of the game, tetherball. For those who might be unfamiliar with the game of tether ball, let me briefly explain.

Individual players stand around a tall steel pole. A rope is attached to the top of the pole and on the end of the rope is a ball about the size of a soccer ball. In the game, individuals hit the ball, one way, while other individuals force it to go in the opposite direction. Now that you've got that picture, let's continue. When we imagine the ball moving forcefully through the air, in either direction, we can compare this to chaotic energy, having no real direction or purpose.

Here's where the important part of the analogy comes in. When you are centered with divine consciousness, you become like the steel pole that is the centerpiece for the game of tetherball. You are not affected by which way the ball is going, nor are you affected by the people hitting the ball. You are centered, grounded and strong in your position. This may seem like a silly analogy to use, yet the life around us can be rather chaotic at times, just like the ball flying around the pole in the game of tetherball. As you learn to master the changes in your reactions more and more, you will find that any chaotic energy you meet will come into balance at a much faster rate. You become the direct force that affects the energy around you. The more you choose powerfully positive reactions or simply no reaction, the more your life will gravitate toward peace, leaving you centered, grounded, and strong in your position. In a way it may feel like a weight has been lifted off of your shoulders, as you allow others to step into accountability for themselves.

As an additional note, through this shift, you may find yourself simply removing yourself from chaotic energy, having no real interest in involving yourself in such things. Your focus will tend to be more on situations that resonate with inner peace and conscious inner growth. Keep in mind that this shift does not mean that you have stopped caring about others. You simply understand that individuals are on their own paths of awakening no matter what that might look like externally. You have gradually learned to see the perfection within the so-called imperfections of life. It's about letting go of control and letting go of judgements and letting go of the ego's position which tends to place everyone in a prison of chaotic emotion. You are setting yourself free and at the same time, giving others the opportunity to do the same if they so choose to shift their own reactions toward life.

Chapter 34

Balancing Changes in Reactions

As you move more and more into understanding your ability to maintain your center and your inner peace, situations may arise that challenge your once typical reactions. Whatever you do, don't loose heart. As you learn to become master over your reactions, your life will become a masterpiece itself. Some ways to help support you in balancing your reactions are the following:

1. Step into Acceptance: Unexpected situations occur in all of our lives. You can count on it, so practicing acceptance can be helpful. Acceptance really is practicing the art of honoring your own experiences as well as the experiences of others. It is placing the harsh hammer of judgement aside. Pure acceptance means letting go of control of how you think that things need to be or ought to be. Keep in mind that the acceptance must first begin with you. When we accept ourselves perfectly, it invites the energy of trust to move into all situations. Acceptance can also be expanded into the energy of non-resistance. If we resist what is showing up, it will more than likely expand the energy of that situation. What we resist will persist. What we accept we will perfect.

2. Practice Bringing Yourself to Center: Shifting your reactions to being a loving observer takes conscious and consistent practice when unexpected situations occur. For instance, a situation that may slightly trigger your emotions may need some fine tuning on your part. If you find yourself being triggered or even slightly reacting with negative emotion or resistance, there are a couple of helpful exercises that can support you in shifting the energy to a more positive or neutral position. You can begin by envisioning the person who is struggling with a challenge working it out in their own way. See them mastering the problem, much like a child mastering tying their shoes for the first time. You can also envision the individual or situation surrounded by the transformative energy of love. See the energy of love transmuting any difficult energy and transforming it for the highest good of all. These are two techniques that I have personally used and have seen miracles occur without speaking a word or getting entangled in chaotic energy. As a side note, one thing to keep in mind is the more consistent you can be with these exercises, the more the transformative energy will build around the individual of concern or situation. See yourself as rays of sunlight shining light upon the situation and trust that you, yes you, are that powerful.

3. Practice Patience: When we highlight the word patience, we invite the energy of divine timing to come in and to work its magic on situations that require time to work themselves out. Time is a gift and practicing patience within that time displays a deeper trust that all is working out, even if on the physical level things may appear otherwise. An analogy for this concept can be understood as you do a simple visualization with me. Imagine a timeline above you that has a beginning and an end, which represents linear time. It is limited by its very nature and scope. You can see the beginning and end, yet nothing beyond that, which automatically erases the eternal possibilities. Now,

if you would take that line and imagine it curling itself end to end forming a circle, which has no beginning and no end. It is timeless and the energy of possibilities moving around that circle is boundless. Just by simply changing your view on the line once presented to you, you can change outcomes. Now, imagine that circle of energy being placed around a situation that needs time to work itself out. The rotation of energy will move accordingly until all comes into balance. Your job is to go into deeper trust and to send positive energy to that circle, trusting that all is coming into balance as you remain centered in your light.

4. Choose Love: Ultimately, changing the way you react to situations is consciously choosing love. Perhaps a pertinent question you could ask yourself when faced with a challenging situation is, "How would love see this?" By asking this question, you are in essence asking your higher self for truth of all things to be revealed and healed. In conclusion, the most important thing that you can do in shifting former reactions to new ways of thinking and being is to simply keep an open-heart revolving around all situations. It is after all the most powerful part of you – one that has the ability to move mountains.

Chapter 35

Indicator 10 - Letting Go of Judgement

As you are moving into spiritual maturity, you are beginning to feel a deep love for all of humanity. You are moving out of spiritual forgetfulness and into the energy realms of seeing beyond the veil. Some may wonder what the veil is and for some this may be a whole new concept to consider, however, bear with me.

The veil is exactly what your soul is housed in, meaning your physical body. The veil or body acts as a vehicle allowing each of us to experience what it's like to live in a dense, physical reality with well-equipped senses like taste, sight, sound, touch, and smell. As mentioned earlier, the physical body is currently vibrating at a lower rate than our spiritual bodies, so the two are not yet in coherence or harmony with each other, however, through time and patience, this can change.

You may be wondering what the veil or body has to do with letting go of judgement so I will explain through a practical analogy to bring clarity. Imagine if you had a friend who had been knocked unconscious and put in the hospital to recover from their injury, but most importantly, recovering their memory. In such a situation, you would visit the friend and share stories of their life to remind them of what their life was like prior to their amnesia. Every bit of information you provide could potentially trigger a forgotten memory. In time the memories would begin to resurface putting together the puzzle pieces once lost within the hidden spaces of the mind.

Likewise, I suppose you could say that everyone on the planet to some degree or another has a case of amnesia, but only in this case, it's what I call, spiritual amnesia. I have often said that humans are in a deep state of spiritual amnesia and it's only a matter of time that each of us wakes up to the truth of who we truly are. Part of the purpose of creating this material is to support you in that awakening process.

As we begin to wake up through ascension symptoms or the indicators of our soul's progression, the veil of our dense physical bodies will become energetically lighter, transforming the physical DNA structures of what we know as our earth body. As this occurs, our intricate connection with the divine creation of the God within will awaken to the truth of divine love. The egoic mind's illusionary pedestal will be cast aside and in turn, the divine mind will ultimately see through the illusion of the veil of the body that has kept most asleep in the corridors of forgetfulness. We will begin to look past the cocoon of the limiting titles or roles that humans have awkwardly wrapped themselves up in. We will step out of the imprisonment of judgement and instead step into a space of pure unadulterated acceptance, forgiveness, and grace, understanding that every role played in the eternal scheme has been divinely orchestrated by all, from eternity through eternity, and for the highest good of all. We will break free of what we have always been . . . love it its purest form.

So here you are, now learning to let go of judgment, understanding that each soul is experiencing what they need to expand the corridors of their divine heart, which is the greatest expression of their soul. No matter how situations may appear on the surface of life, you have found yourself having a change of heart. You no longer judge what you once judged. You have stepped into a deeper trust, knowing that all things are in divine timing, divine order, and divine purpose. You have come to understand that everything is connected energetically and the best position that you can take is to extend love, compassion, understanding, and forgiveness to yourself and all. You have also learned a deeper sense of self-love, which will in turn naturally remove judgment from your reality. You are moving into pure gratitude which casts out all positions of judgment. As you continue to step into a space of non-judgment, it honestly lifts a tremendous burden off of you. It also sets others free energetically to orchestrate and navigate the perfect outcomes for them.

To demonstrate a simple analogy, you could see judgment as a web like energy field that casts further restrictions on others as you project your thoughts or words onto others. When you step away from the tendency of judgment, you stop casting a web of restrictions upon others. How is it that you can form such a web? It is because you have that same web cast upon yourself as well. Letting go of judgment sets you and others free to be the best versions of themselves.

Every day we are presented with opportunities to resurrect ourselves through the choice of forgiveness. When we truly forgive, we truly forget who we thought we were. This dissolves any supposed impurities within the body even down to the smallest particle of imbalance, physically, emotionally, mentally, and spiritually. Any dense or dark energies are invited to awaken to redeeming light that is filled with infinite grace, pointing to rebirth and the resurrection within. The truth is, forgiveness of self is the only real thing that needs forgiving. When we realize that the self is connected to everything, that forgiveness is applied to everything. Through this compassionate act toward the divided self, reconciliation between the mind and the heart begin to build a bridge of complete unity, and remembrance of the infinite, divine self. When we are able to master this mystery of self-forgiveness, it is then that the merging of physical and spiritual DNA can ignite the energy of ascension within our collective heart.

"Throughout the eternal scope of life, may we awaken to the divine expression of every soul experiencing the infinitely divine possibilities of love's potential all around them."

Leslie Paramore

Chapter 36

Balancing Letting Go of Judgement

Obviously letting go of judgment doesn't happen overnight. It is a continual invitation on a daily basis to free all from the energy of restriction that binds a soul and prevents us from knowing who we are. It's quite an undertaking, however, not impossible. Some helpful tools to support you in letting go of judgment are the following suggestions.

1. Be Aware of Judgement: A powerful way to let go of judgment is to first be aware of when you are judging a person or situation. Judgment often has a projection, opinion, or emotion attached to it. Let's look at an example by examining two statements that focus on the same situation.

Here's the first statement. *"There are many homeless individuals in the city."* This statement is merely an observation noting the number of homeless people. There is no opinion or projection of emotion attached to it. Now, here's the second statement. *"There are many homeless individuals in the city because they are lazy and simply don't want to work."* Do you see how this second is a judgment or projection of someone's perceptions based on their own emotions? It is helpful to practice recognizing how many times you find yourself judging things.

It might surprise you initially, however, as you continue to be aware of it, you will let go more and more. Practice shifting the sentence from judgment to observation. Turn it around to turn the energy around.

2. Practice Forgiveness: One of the best ways to let go of judgement is to practice forgiveness. Now, allow me to explain this in terms of ascension views. Forgiveness is "for-giving-all" the highest form of spiritual healing available to mankind, in which divine love penetrates its light into the dark corridors of spiritual forgetfulness. Forgiveness says, "I choose to see our light through the illusion of our darkness. Forgiveness is about waking up to the light within, excusing the fact that any-thing in the external world ever had power over us." When you forgive you are in essence, releasing any binding energy that keeps your heart in the dark. With forgiveness, you can then invite the energy of your heart to open, radiating light to any-thing that can keep you from waking up to the truth of who you truly are. The pain of past experiences no longer occupies the spaces of your mind or your heart.

3. Live in the Moment of Right Now: When you are truly heart-centered in your life, you can live in a powerful space called, "Right Now." In this space, a calm energy is able to sur-round you, no matter what chaos may be all around you. There is an unquenchable peace that speaks a still silence into your heart, that all is well, even if it may appear on the surface like it's not. Living in the moment of Right Now, is going deeper into you. Deeper into trust. Deeper into light. Deeper into one-ness. When you are living in the moment of right now, there is no past where your mind can get lost in a vast array of negative memories. When you are living in the moment of right now, there is no future where you dream needlessly of things that are already yours. The moment of right now is the most peace-

ful, yet powerful space you can be. As you practice being there, life will transform right before your eyes, and you will begin to see beyond the illusion of your thoughts and into the truth of your heart. The truth that love is simply in the process of re-membering itself through every person you encounter.

4. Choose to See Healing: In every instant in life, we are given a choice. We can choose love or fear, forgiveness, or re-venge, or gratitude over regret. Life can be filled with chal-lenges or opportunities, depending on how you choose to look at it. Choose to see healing to move past hurt feelings. This practice can be applied to a person, situation, or event. We can choose to see a situation or person working their way to heal-ing through their experiences. See them conquering the obsta-cle. See them overcoming their doubt, anger, or fear. See them in their true form, void of spiritual forgetfulness. This is a pow-erful way to help support individuals who are struggling with life, including yourself. The power of thought and emotion put together can move stagnant, chaotic, or stuck energy in any situation. The important thing to note is that as you practice this visualization technique, be patient. The physical world is a dense frequency, and it takes time to get through it in order to elevate the potential outcomes for all concerned. Be mind-ful of your own limiting thoughts and personal projections and attachments to outcomes, as this can slow down the process of healing.

When you practice these four suggestions consistently, you will be remarkably surprised at the results as you let go of judgement right now.

Chapter 37

Indicator 11 - Letting Go of Fear

We very much live in a fear-based world, where every day we are bombarded with media that paints a picture of doom and gloom seeded both within our minds and our hearts. Much of our media highlights things in the world that are fearful, judgmental, shameful, or harmful, as they parade the latest story across our television or computer screens. Of course, much of what they portray is a ridiculously small percentage of the negative things that humans do to each other. It's like looking at life through a dark straw seeing only a narrow and tainted view of life. If we are tied into it, life can have us sitting on the edge of our seats, with our mind placed on high alert, waiting, and watching for the next unhealthy adrenaline rush to invade our bodies.

Much of our movie and entertainment industry is also based on fear and violence or some kind of suspense or drama, and in some distorted way, people get a chemical high from subjecting themselves to painful stimuli. Fear-based energy can be addictive, even if it's uncomfortable. In time, with repeated exposure, we become numb to things that once spoke warnings to our spiritual conscience.

As you begin to awaken, your conscious self now becomes less tolerant of such things, and no longer wishes to get taken away through the fears and dramas of life. You wake up to the fact that the physical world had some type of hypnotic trance on you that kept you asleep to who you truly are. You finally begin to see through the trickery of fear-based energy created by mankind which has always kept you small and limited in your experiences. In essence, your divine self is now rising above the collective fear you have been entangled in for most of your life. You also understand that those caught up in a world of fear have simply lost themselves in a temporary state of spiritual amnesia. Their awakening will come in due time, just as your time has now come.

Through your awakening you now find yourself creating higher states of consciousness such as peace, joy, love, and abundance. You find yourself associating with experiences that will magnify the best in you and those around you. You let go of limiting beliefs and see the best possible outcomes unfolding for all concerned. The lines of division are now fading, as you understand your divine connection to everything and everyone around you. Being the presence of love is now your primary focus as the ways of the old world of worry becomes blurry, out of focus, moving further and further from your reality. These new feelings of empowerment set the stage where you get to be the author of your reality, no longer giving your power away to external forces of limiting fear. In time, you will see the silver lining in every human's cloudy experience including your own, for a perfect love casts out all fear.

Keep in mind that letting go of fear does not mean you lack empathy or concern for yourself or others. It simply means that you are choosing to see the bigger picture that we are all creating together as a human race. Letting go of fear requires you to move into deeper trust that there is a grand design and path woven through each and every soul. Every soul must evolve through personal growth and birth the truth of love from within.

"When one claims the courage to walk through the illusionary walls of fear, it is there they will discover the infinite joy of their soul, welcoming them home to the infinite path of divine love awakening. "

- Leslie Paramore

Chapter 38

Balancing Letting Go of Fear

Letting go of fear can take time to master especially when you have had a lifetime of conditioning, however, the following are some practical things you can do to support you as you awaken to the love within you.

1. Visualize Healing Outcomes: As you move throughout your life, now leaving all fear behind you, you may occasionally be faced with the old belief systems of fear as you move forward into personal spiritual empowerment. This is your opportunity to reaffirm that fear no longer has power over you by seeing fear-based situations resurrecting and transforming into positive outcomes. This is a technique that I have used many times, with amazing results. For example, someone you know is having relationship issues. In that moment, instead of focusing on the emotional struggle between the parties involved, simply visualize the persons working out the issue, trusting that all conflict eventually gets resolved. See it as an opportunity for the people involved to work through deeper issues that are supporting them in their own waking up experience.

2. Be A Calm Presence: When chaos arises, a calm, confident and reassuring spiritual presence can diffuse any physical
situation. A Spiritual Master can remain calm in all situations,
cutting their way through limiting boundaries of fear. You can
stand in your spiritual power as a new master in training, by re-
maining calm in the midst of life's unpredictable storms. This
calm energy can be found when you connect with the universal consciousness of God, which is love itself. This is where
peace lives as you remain calm. If you witness any tense situations outside of you, breathing in calm through your crown
chakra as you connect with Universal energy is a good meditation practice. As you expand the calm energy within you, see
calm waves move outward beyond your body, creating ripples
of positive change all around you. The best way to master this
technique is to practice it daily.

3. Divorce Yourself from Fear: Letting go of fear, often
means you need to let go of the things that were creating the
energy of fear in your life in the first place. It's a conscious decision that you will be glad you're making, as it makes room
for a life filled with peace, joy, love, and abundance. Let's face
it, if you wish to refurnish a room to upgrade its value, I'm
sure you would agree that you must first get rid of the clutter
that is getting in the way of the fresh new look. You will recall when we spoke of something invasive that projects fearful
energy into your life on a daily basis. Like a thief in the night,
it gains access to your subconscious mind imprinting it with
fear-based energy, which in turn, clutters your space. The projections of television and most of the programs offered are like
that old, worn out, cluttered room we spoke of earlier. You can
think of your divine mind as the new room you wish to refurnish with peace, joy, love, and abundance. Think of how it will
feel to release yourself from fear, as you clear your mind of the
cluttered programming you once subjected yourself to. Imag-

ine how light that will feel, not to mention freeing. In short, I encourage you to reconsider what you are placing in the room of your new mind. Refrain from watching television or movie projections that are based in the energy of fear. I also invite you to monitor what fear-based television projections are being placed within the mind of your children.

"Take flight into the unknown corridors of your soul, where nothing is impossible and dreams magically become your reality. Awaken to your light, dear soul. The morning of your beautiful resurrection has come!"

- Leslie Paramore

Chapter 39

Indicator 12 - Magnification of The Seven Senses

There are some much like myself, who have experienced a magnification of the senses which actually include seven senses, which are sight, sound, taste, touch, smell, your sixth sense of the divine mind, which is intuition, and finally your seventh sense, which is your divine heart. As you shift in spiritual consciousness it only stands to reason, additional aspects of you will shift as well. With your new upgrade into becoming more conscious, you will experience not only spiritual changes, but also physical changes, emotional changes, and mental changes.

Earlier in this material we mentioned how the integration of your spiritual DNA and physical DNA would eventually become one complimentary system. As your circuitry systems turn on within your spiritual DNA, this shift can also magnify your senses. Your sensory systems are now becoming much more sensitive to external and internal stimuli. Keep in mind that not everyone will have all senses magnified. For some, magnification may be isolated to one or two senses, while with other individuals it may encompass all seven senses mentioned before.

Let's briefly cover some changes you might expect to experience as a more conscious being moving toward ascension.

Exploring Your Seven Primary Senses

Taste: With respect to your sense of taste, you may suddenly begin to taste unnatural chemicals within processed foods and tap water. At first this may be alarming, and you may even shy away from foods that you once enjoyed, however, I urge you to listen to the feedback that your body is offering you as you move forward into new awareness for the healthy upgrades of your new body.

Touch: In the areas of magnification of touch, your skin or body may feel more sensitive to touch. This shift can create different outcomes for individuals. The sense of touch may become more pleasurable, which can increase your ability to connect with the sensation of touch or you may have extreme sensitivities in being touched in any way. You may find yourself avoiding any physical contact with people, including things like hugging, hand holding, kissing or sexual activity. These experiences will balance themselves in time. Trust that your body is making the necessary upgrades in intelligently profound ways.

Sound: As we examine the magnification of your sense of sound, you may find that your ability to be around large crowds is simply intolerable for you right now. Perhaps at one time you could filter out the noise and now noise feels like long fingernails going down a chalkboard, with external sounds piercing your ears. You may also have a change in your music preferences. Tones and pitches are more easily discerned and your ability to be more cognizant of words sung or spoken will take on a whole new meaning as you attune yourself to your new energy body. At times high- or low-pitched tones may be heard in your internal ear, which is also known as ringing in the ear. Be reassured that this ringing is an internal communication activated by your spiritual DNA which speaks messages into your cellular blueprint for cellular shifts. Sound is powerful and your new magnification revolving around sound and your sensitivities to it, are creating changes within you.

Sight: As we explore the magnification of sight, I must say that this sense can be one of the most extreme experiences, as much of what we experience in the physical world relies on our sight and the information filtered through to our brains. For myself, the magnification of sight was especially difficult as there were times that going into a store or anywhere public felt too visually overwhelming. Someone who experiences magnification of their sight will see every aspect of visual stimuli all at once. For a simple example, when a person looks at a carpet, they will not just see a carpet, they will see every fiber of every strand within the carpet and also, every color. Like all shifts, this too will find its center point of balance.

Smell: As we continue to examine the possible shifts in the senses, we would also like to address your sense of smell. Most of us are aware that a pregnant woman will often have sensitivities to smells that never bothered her before becoming pregnant, yet the life inside of her has created energy shifts. Through this process of awakening to ascension, we too are pregnant with new energy making its way through our systems, to evolve into a new being. Your sense of smell may change more in the areas of things that are harmful to your physical body such as chemicals used for cleaning etc. You may also be hypersensitive to the smells of foods that have gone bad.

The Divine Mind: Bear with us as we cover two more senses that may be a bit more unfamiliar to you. The sixth sense that is often magnified through conscious awakening is the divine mind, which is linked to your spiritual intuition. Intuition occurs when you become more connected to the divine energies of spirit or your inner knowing, which is what your soul carries within its DNA. When your spiritual DNA activates the pineal gland located at the back portion of the brain, your third eye awakens your ability to see or sense beyond the physical experience. This experience of magnification can be a little intimidating as you are learning to see life on a deeper level.

The Divine Heart: Finally we highlight the magnification of the divine heart, which is where the intelligence of your infinite soul rests. The divine heart is different from your physical heart although the two energies are seeking to merge into a new heart as you work toward ascension. The divine heart houses the energy of love which is eternally infinite and always expanding in consciousness. If you did not have this spark of loving divinity within you, you would not have the ability to experience yourself in physical form. Think of the divine heart as the battery that charges your vehicle running all the systems both physically and spiritually. Magnification of the divine heart leads to deeper abilities to love all of humanity regardless of their spiritual amnesia. The divine heart knows its power and worth and it is through this activated energy that miracles are realized.

Chapter 40

Balancing Magnification of The Seven Senses

When life around us is suddenly being magnified, through our seven senses, it can feel overwhelming and can definitely take some time to adjust to, however, trust that all aspects of you are equipped with an intelligent design that is orchestrating outcomes for your highest good. Remember that not all senses will be magnified at once. Most times it's a gradual transition so our physical bodies can make the necessary adjustments. Also keep in mind that these periods of magnification level off from sometimes intense, then transitioning to becoming your new normal. It is our intention that the material provided for support will bring greater clarity and understanding to make these transitional shifts as easy as possible for all concerned. Let's look at some helpful suggestions that you can begin implementing right now revolving around each of the seven senses.

1. Magnification of Physical Sight: One of the best ways to balance your magnification of sight is to simply rest your vision. This resting can prevent feelings of being overwhelm-

ingly stimulated, which can then lead to feelings of anxiety. You can balance your vision by doing some of the following: If you are feeling overwhelmed visually, close your eyes and simply breathe deep when it is safe to do so. You can also create a calm environment that is visually balanced and less stimulating. Ideally this space can be your entire living area or a Zen corner where you can relax your visual energy. Engage in meditation where you can focus on one object like a burning candle to bring you back to your calm center. When your vision is heightened, avoid busy places like stores, parties, outdoor areas, or anything that could create feelings of visual anxiousness. And finally, take time to connect with nature and ground to the frequencies of mother earth and also the frequencies of a Higher Source that can support you through this process.

2. Magnification of Taste: We live in a world that is highly motivated by food. It's a multibillion-dollar industry. We are catered to and marketed to on so many levels it's difficult to trace the steps it takes to get you the consumer to cave into the pressure of the marketing mania revolving around food. Meticulous packaging of products appeals to the eyes, and it seems that some unseen force urges you to place the item into your shopping cart. You get the food item home, cook it up and not surprisingly, it looks nothing like the way it was displayed on the box that it came in. One bite of the item and your taste buds may send the signal that what you just placed in your mouth was an insult to your high vibrational pallet. Do you get the picture? As you shift in consciousness, your relationship with food may change based on the fact that you may gradually begin to taste the chemicals in the food. You may go from processed foods to preferring salads and soups. You may transition from eating meat to no meat at all. The only counsel I have for you regarding this is to trust your tastes buds. Be more conscious when eating and commit to eating foods that res-

onate with your body. There is no room for self-sabotage when it comes to food. Eat with a heart filled with thanksgiving and digest the rest with conscious choices.

3. Magnification of Sound: Our ears are like funnels that filter sound waves through them to be interpreted throughout our body. Sound has the ability to affect our bodies even down to the cellular level. In fact, even our cells make sounds through the respiration of the cell. Sound has the ability to move matter through energy. A simple example of this would be a technique known as, cymatics where vibrational frequencies manifested as sound are seen as form, which is usually displayed on a solid metal surface. Salt is placed on a flat metal surface, as a tone is played. The higher the frequency, the more intricate the pattern. I encourage you to look up the experiments of cymatics. When your sense of sound is heightened, you may need to adjust the way you expose yourself to sound. Some things you can do to support yourself through this is to pay deeper attention to sound. Pay attention to what sounds cause you irritation. Pay attention to the sounds that create inner peace. Avoid or limit your time in places that have too much sound, or a mixture of sounds. You know your tolerance levels more than anyone, so it will be up to you to listen intently to the sounds all around you and make the necessary adjustments to support you through this shift. As an additional note, some individuals may increase their ability to hear beyond the physical reality and into the spiritual realms. This gift is called, clairaudience. The sound you hear is not actually physically heard, but intuitively heard. If this is occurring with you, it can be startling and can cause you to feel like you are losing your mind. Be reassured that such is not the case. We will cover this phenomenon in greater detail later in this material, so until then listen to the part of you that knows deep inner truth.

4. Magnification of Touch: For every magnification surfacing, there comes the opportunity to find balance within it. The hypersensitivity to touch can be so extreme that for some even the feeling of certain types of clothing against their skin can be irritating. If you find yourself being hypersensitive to any form of touch, don't lose heart as you bring balance into this area of your life. There are many ways you can bring balance for this particular sensitivity. Here are a few suggestions. Set boundaries for yourself and honor those boundaries by expressing them to others. If you prefer not to hug or have various forms of touch, it's okay to express that to others. Grounding with the earth can also support you with easing the sensitivities of touch. If having your feet in the grass bothers you while grounding, place them in water, or touch a tree. Either will support the energies to balance out your sensitivities to touch. You can also balance these hypersensitivities by having an Epsom salt bath to help diffuse the tension within your body. Also, finding things to comfort you while distancing yourself from physical touch can benefit you, like wrapping yourself up in a warm blanket or cuddling a teddy bear. Be reassured that these sensitivities, although they may appear to be physical, are more than likely derived from energetic sensitivities while you are undergoing a transformational shift between your body and spirit. You may have experienced someone getting within close proximity to you where it felt quite uncomfortable. We all have an energy bubble around us called an aura and those sensitive to touch are most likely experiencing some physical and spiritual integrations within themselves. It's not surprising that they intuitively shy away from anything that might interfere with that integration. Keep honoring yourself as you move through this magnification of touch and at the very least, give yourself a hug. You've got this!

5. Magnification of Smell: It is said that we are attracted to others through hormones subconsciously released from our bodies called, pheromones. Many of our decisions in life are based on our sense of smell. If someone smells bad, we tend to distance ourselves from them. If you're looking to purchase a home, and there's a cow pasture beside it, you may reconsider. If a certain food smells good, you will more than likely purchase it. The magnification of smell can be a good thing when we tune into it. In one such case involving myself, I was sitting in a restaurant when someone at my table had ordered fish. The moment the fish was set down on the table, my gag reflex kicked in as I smelled the rotten odor that immediately permeated the area. Surprisingly, I was the only one who could smell it, with the exception of a friend who could faintly smell the steaming rotten flesh of the half-baked fish. With my repulsed reaction, and verbal insistence, the fish was quickly taken away to be replaced with one that was fresh. Although an unpleasant experience, in that particular case, I was thankful that I may have saved someone from food poisoning. Let's briefly mention what actions could help support this shift in your sense of smell. Your sense of smell and taste go together, so the same counsel or suggestions for support is being offered. Use your discretion and trust your sense of smell, just as you trust your sense of taste. For instance, if certain household cleaning chemicals bother you, you may need to change your buying habits for a more natural, odorless cleaner. You can apply the same methods to food or any other choices you are faced with based on your sense of smell. When it comes to making good decisions for your new life, follow your nose.

6. Magnification of Your Divine Mind: We have all experienced intuition, however, most often those keen insights occur in sporadic spurts. For instance, the phone rings and you know who it is before answering, or you've been thinking of

someone for a week and then suddenly you run into them at the grocery store. Also, perhaps you can perceive what someone is thinking before they speak it. These spurts of intuition may come and go depending on what's going on in our lives and how distracted we may be. There are many examples that we could highlight, however, these are sufficient for what we are conveying at this moment.

In sharing information about the divine mind, some may mistake it for the natural or physical mind. For the purposes of this material, we will define the divine mind as the supernatural part of you where your connection and receptivity to God and Spirit resides. The intuition of the third eye chakra is governed by the divine mind; however, something needs to happen first, before the third eye awakens. The spiritual mechanics of how the divine mind works is completely fascinating. Your third eye chakra, located between your brow, is connected to the pineal gland; a small pinecone shaped gland located deep in the center portion of the brain between the left and right hemispheres. Your pineal gland is said to be about the size of a grain of rice and acts as a spiritual receptor or antennae that is connected to your third eye. As communication and connection with God, Spirit, or Divinity moves through your crown chakra located at the top of your head, divine energy activates the pineal gland and awakens the third eye chakra, giving you your keen sense of intuition. With this connection, the divine mind is then activated, allowing you to see through the veil of the physical world and into the spiritual world which is invisible to most. The magnification of the divine mind can open up a whole new world for you on so many levels. You may begin to see things not visible to the naked eye, like auras, energy, spirits, angels, fairies, and things that humans would call mystical or unexplained phenomena. This magnification can be startling if you don't know what the possibilities are. You may also have increased abilities like extra sensory perception, telepathy, and telekinesis to name a few. Magnification of the divine mind is part of your awakening process, so again, trust that you are not losing your mind, you are simply gaining a new and improved one. Some things you can do through this process is to stay grounded, meaning, stay in your body and connect with the earth. You can also spend time in calming meditation. Get plenty of rest when you can. Also, if this magnification is too much for you at any given moment, you can ask that the energy be dialed back a bit. Remember, you're not alone in this process of awakening to ascension. You have plenty of support in the spiritual realms where light beings, guides, angels, and many others are aware of your awakening. If something you don't understand shows up, ask what the purpose of it is. For instance, if you begin to see auras, that's great, but look to expand your spiritual wisdom by asking what the purpose of the experience is for? Is it leading you somewhere? Asking will always expand the divine mine, so don't be shy, ask and you shall always receive.

7. Magnification of Your Divine Heart: Everyone knows that feelings of love are associated with the heart space. Your heart puts out electrical messages that communicate and govern the entire body, including the brain. You have a physical heart; however, you also hold the energy of the soul or the divine heart within you. The spark of intelligent light that keeps your body alive is the energy of your divine heart. This divine energy is connected to both your physical DNA as well as your Spiritual DNA, communicating and orchestrating the eventual merging of both bodies. The expanding energy of the divine heart or life force within you holds the intelligence of God and your connection to all that is. As this power center magnifies, your ability to truly feel love without condition increases. It can be a magical place as you see through the current phys-

ical limitations of humanity and into the heart of every soul. You know that your divine heart is expanding when you begin to have a feeling of deep connection with everything around you. You feel an emotion of indescribable love for all, and at times it can bring you to tears. At times, you may even look at another and see a portion of yourself. Perhaps you have felt these things or are beginning to awaken this portion of you. The illusion of division is fading and the merging of all that you are is beginning. All magnification of your senses are linked to the divine heart and its connection to God, which is infinite, eternal love. This truly is a beautiful path of oneness within you. As the merging of the divine mind and the divine heart connect with the ultimate Source of God, it creates a balanced union of reconciliation and communion. Through this gradual shift, all things one separated become one with God. Some ways that you can support the magnification of your divine heart are the following:

1. Practice Feeling Emotion: Practice showing compassion and empathy for all, individually and collectively, including yourself. Compassion and empathy have the ability to see the highest possibilities or outcomes for every soul as you support through love and understanding.

2. Ask To Receive: Ask for divine support as you seek ways of experiencing life in a way that the divine love of God would see it. Often through the human heart we are limited, yet through the divine heart, we can begin to experience the path of true unadulterated love. Empty your cup of human opinions or judgements and let the influence of divinity fill it with clarity, compassion, and love for all.

3. Forgive One And All: Open your heart to forgiveness for self and others, understanding that each soul has its sacred

journey to ascend to the divine consciousness of God. All is in divine timing, order, and purpose. Every experience is designed to bring every soul closer to the truth within, unveiling a period of spiritual forgetfulness. This is why one of the Divine Masters named, Jesus said, "Father forgive them for they know not what they do."

4. Heal With Intentions: Live with the intention of healing yourself mentally, emotionally, physically, and spiritually, through the seven beautiful senses you have been given. Trust that as you do so, your awakening to ascension will unfold in a divine design. Set clear intentions for living a beautiful life filled with beautiful opportunities, consciously seeing the world coming together as one heart beating in harmony and unison.

5. Get Closer: Gather with like hearted individuals for support and learning. At times when you are awakening these parts of yourself, you can feel even more isolated as you move further and further away from the conditioning of the world that you have been living in for most of your life. The gathering of like hearted individuals creates an energy of oneness and connection.

6. Visualize Complete Healing: Practice seeing and feeling beyond the illusion of this world. See all as healed and whole, all as one, all as love. This is truth and the truth shall surely set you free. Remember we have forgotten who we are, and, in that forgetfulness, we have been wrapped up in our roles and titles. We are all love working on remembering itself through every experience presented to us. See the world in perfection and all humans awakening to ascension.

"As you search the deepest parts of your divine mind and heart, it is there that you will discover a beautiful communion between the two. For these two parts of you were never meant to be divided, but to come together in one harmonious song."

Leslie Paramore

Chapter 41

Indicator 13 - Increased Emotional Awareness

Most people have been taught to suppress emotions either during childhood or sometime throughout their lifetime. We've been conditioned to wear invisible masks that hide how we truly feel. At some point in our lives, we have all put on a happy face for everyone to see, while the way we truly felt inside may have been quite the opposite emotion. The suppression of emotion has long influenced how we have learned to navigate our way through life. The emotional suppression is particularly evident on the masculine side and often begins during childhood, through well-meaning parents trying to prepare their children for life. In the past, or even today in some cases, boys have been taught not to cry or to toughen up, while girls may be scolded or not taken seriously for expressing anger. Experiences of emotional suppression may not the same for everyone, however, rest assured, we have all suppressed emotion at one time or another.

The emotional suppression you have experienced is a survival mechanism and most times, powerful emotions are suppressed due to fears. As you awaken to increased emotional awareness, the lid of suppression is beginning to come off. You may become more aware or in touch with the emotions that have been suppressed over the years. Often individuals who are waking up to their emotions are doing so due to arousal of pain or discomfort within their body. Because emotion is energy carried in the body throughout our life experiences, negative emotions can create energy blockages within the body. These blockages can cause the body to be in pain or can lead to the development of eventual illness or disease when not dealt with. After extensive medical testing, with no real answers, individuals are intuitively led to go deeper into themselves for the answers that have been buried in emotion for an exceptionally long time. When you are awakening you no longer wish to suppress very deep emotions that have caused you to feel trapped, heavy, or depressed. In many cases, depression is linked to the repression of emotions.

If you've ever cooked food in a pot called, a pressure cooker, you know that the steam builds up with heat to cook the food, but at some point, the steam builds up to the point that it must be released. In a sense, your body can act like a pressure cooker as well. The emotions buried have to be released. As a result, some of you may find yourselves crying more, or even have periods of anger, frustration, anxiety or feelings of exhaustion or depression. Although this can be intensely uncomfortable, these emotions that no longer vibrationally resonate within your body are surfacing from the dark tomb they've been buried in. It's a natural part of your awakening, healing, and spiritual ascension. Trust the process of your own awakening, and rise to greater possibilities for your unlimited life.

Chapter 42

Balancing Increased Emotional Awareness

This time period of emotional awareness can last several months to several years, depending on each person's ability to acknowledge, validate, and let go of the emotions that have been suppressed. The following suggestions are offered to support you in processing and releasing emotions that are no longer in harmonic resonance with your body.

1. Give Yourself Permission to Feel: Oftentimes unexpected emotions may arise and not always at the most convenient times. Perhaps you find yourself crying for no apparent reason. Due to your lack of understanding, your first reaction will be to suppress like you've always done. If emotion arises, give yourself permission to feel in order to release it and heal.

2. Participate in Guided Meditations: There are guided meditations that focus on healing your inner child. Guided meditations can lead you on a journey of healing where you are invited to connect with the energies of your divine mind and heart to create a balanced life. As an adult, you now have the power and choice to heal your inner child. Meditation can be a

powerful way to connect with your highest self, which is connected with God or divine love, the infinite healer.

3. Create a Releasing Ceremony for Yourself: A releasing ceremony is a way to create closure and healing for yourself. It is symbolic of burying the old you and inviting the new you to be resurrected into your new life. To begin, write down something that comes to you that you are now ready to release from your life. This could be a past event that created pain during any time of your life from childhood on to adulthood. The experience that surfaces in your memory is the one ready to be released.

Your statement may go something like the following examples: *"I now release the pain of feeling sad about . . ."* or *"I now release the feelings of anger about . . . "* or *"I now release the feelings of feeling worried about . . ."* Once you have written down the thing you are ready to release, say it out loud. Afterwards, be sure to express gratitude for the lessons or wisdom learned. You can then tear up the paper, dig a hole in the ground, and burn the paper. Once all paper has been burned, you may cover it over with dirt and consider it buried and released. You can then offer a prayer of gratitude if desired.

The final step in the releasing ceremony involves stepping into your personal power and writing the new emotions and situations down that you are now creating. Some examples could be . . .

"I now receive with joy my newly created life as I . . ."
"I now receive with gratitude . . ."
"I now receive the strength to . . ."

Keep in mind, there is no right or wrong way to participate in a releasing ceremony. Perhaps this suggestion may inspire you to create your own releasing ceremony of a different nature.

4. Get Healing Support When Needed: There are many loving and inspired healers who can support you in feeling and releasing your emotions. It can take time, yet the more you meet your feelings in the center of your heart, the greater empowerment you will feel. I personally have supported many individuals on the journey of remembering their true identity and claiming a new life for themselves.

Although my passion revolves around empowering others, rest assured, I too have experienced my own awakening symptoms which has ultimately led me in creating this material for you. It is my sincere desire that the information offered assists you in navigating your way to your personal awakening and eventual ascension.

Chapter 43

Indicator - 14
Increased
Sensitivity Toward
Self and Others

As you awaken, your awareness expands to your divine connection with those around you. At one time it appeared that life revolved around your own personal experiences and choices and maybe you didn't give any real consideration to how your choices may have affected others, yet as you awaken, things change. We learn that what we call our personal choices do affect others, creating a ripple effect of energy that influences all to some degree or another.

An indicator of your awakening may be increased sensitivity to self and others. As you tune into your direct and indirect connection with those around you, you may find yourself experiencing unusual sensitivities. At times you may consciously or unconsciously absorb energies that are not yours to carry, yet because of this new awareness, you inadvertently create unhealthy boundaries between yourself and your experiences. Understanding your connection to everything can increase your sensitivity, that is, until you are able to increase your capacity to love unconditionally.

Allow us to explain further. When you feel your connection to others, you can actually see them as an unhealed part of yourself. They are in essence a mirror or a reflection that you have attracted into your life for deeper introspection on a subconscious level. What we believe internally, will often be mirrored externally in our experiences with others. The tendency is for most human empaths to absorb or take upon themselves the unhealed emotions or heavy energies of others, because it seems like the nice thing to do, right? This unhealthy tendency is actually volunteering yourself as a martyr and thus engaging yourself in codependent relationships. A codependent relationship is a relationship based on emotional deficiencies within both parties involved. Both parties feel broken to a certain degree, and therefore come together in attempt to be made whole, however, what they don't realize is that their spiritual amnesia makes them forget that they are already whole. When you open yourself up to absorb the energies of others, you are literally giving your power away to the external world, which then has control over your internal circuitry systems.

Part of the sensitivity you may be feeling is designed to wake you up to the capacity of the love within you. At one time, when you thought your choices revolved around you, and only you, you may have been closed off to the sensitivities and the affects your choices had on others. Now through your awakening your conscious mind is awakening. Your sensitivity was designed to be a gift. Someone who is truly tuned into being empathic will extend love and compassion without forming an opinion or judgement on another's experience. They will visualize them as being whole and healed, seeing past the illusion of brokenness.

Instead of playing the role of the martyr, thinking with great determination that you need to carry the emotions of others, why not look at this from a different perspective. Remember the mirror of reflection we mentioned earlier? If you could show up as a mirror for others, what would you like them to see? What beautiful light lies within you that could be reflected for others so that they may see glimpses of their true identity? This approach can be empowering for both you and those you encounter throughout your life.

As a side note, spiritually, we are all awakening together, creating a ripple effect. We have all played roles of the victim, the martyr, the villain and the judge, the jury, and the accuser, yet now in this awakening, we are laying our titles and our roles down and seeing into the heart of what is real. It's okay to be sensitive, but let that beautiful sensitivity awaken itself to the love within all.

"A kind and sensitive heart is a gift to humanity, as it allows the cumbersome and awkward things of this world to pass through the corridors of its love, compassion, and empathy."
- Leslie Paramore

Chapter 44

Balancing Increased Sensitivity Toward Self and Others

Through my spiritual journey, I've learned that sensitivity can be a good thing when received in a way that is balanced and utilized in a way that is love based for everyone involved. Years ago, before I even knew what the word empath was, I used to go out in public and come home heavy and exhausted, not realizing that I was unconsciously acting like a sponge and absorbing the energies all around me. I was socially awkward and incredibly shy. Perhaps you can relate. We are here to suggest that your empathic abilities are a spiritual gift, although some may feel that being an empath is a curse. The following suggestions in this material are designed to help you to awaken your empathic gifts for a new level of appreciation and understanding.

1.Express Gratitude for Your Gift: One of the most powerful things you can step into when you are struggling with something that is difficult to navigate through, is expressing gratitude. When you express gratitude, you literally open your energy field up for greater clarity and awareness. The truth is, empaths were never meant to have bleeding hearts, enable others, or appear as weak people who have no control over their experiences and the energy around them. You are so much more powerful than that! Playing small doesn't serve you, nor does it serve others. Expressing gratitude says, "I am open to learning more about this spiritual gift that I am now learning to master." We suggest that you create a journal of gratitude and write the simple things that you can express gratitude for on a daily basis. Start your entry with these words, "Today I recognize that being an empath is a gift. Today, I am thankful that . . . (I was sensitive and open enough to connect lovingly with a homeless person.) OR today, I am thankful that . . . (I was sensitive and open enough to recognize when I can use some alone time.) Think about it, most people are in such a hurry with life, they often miss beautiful opportunities, yet being an empath leaves you more connected. It's what you do with those connections that matter.

2. Target the Emotion: As an empath in training there may be times where you inadvertently pick up on someone else's emotion and confuse it as your own. If you leave your house feeling great and come back feeling anxious with no apparent cause, chances are the feelings are not yours. This awareness will support you in creating the necessary shifts needed to break old patterns. Once you recognize that you are piggybacking on another's emotion, you can simply set a prayer of intention, releasing it to healing light to be healed, then leave the rest up to the spiritual realms to bring it to completion.

3. Practice Being Love Consciousness: As an empath you have the ability to feel emotions deeply so why not practicing feeling love deeply? A wonderful practice that I engage in on a regular basis is the following. Prior to going out in public, take a few minutes to breathe in the breath of love consciousness in through your crown chakra, inviting it to filter down into your

heart. Once you feel that powerful energy and can visualize it, feel the love consciousness expanding from the center point of your heart in through your entire body. Allow it to continue to expand until it surrounds your entire body. Finally, feel the love surrounding you as you go out into the world as a conscious, loving observer. Practice sending waves of love to anyone you feel impressed to send it to. It can be a happy person, a sad person, an angry person, a frantic person, or anyone at all. You will be amazed at how elevated you feel as you do so.

4. Ask the Purpose for The Gift: As an empath you are gifted with sensitivity, yet have you ever wondered how the gift of sensitivity can be transferred to other areas of your life? For example, I was an extremely sensitive child, with the keen abilities to see through situations and emotions of those much older than myself. For example, I could see through the smile of an adult, and often feel a much deeper emotion that they were trying their best to hide. It was quite confusing and conflicting for me at the time. As my empathic abilities have sharpened, they have proven to be a powerful tool to assist others through my healing work. I can see through conflict in a person's life, dissect it and support them in making sense of why they are going through difficulty. When you ask the purpose for your gifts, you may be surprised where it leads you. Never in a million years would I have ever imagined myself engaged in the work I am doing, yet here I am, an empowered empath, no longer afraid of her shadow. You too can claim that gift.

There are countless ways you will be led to awaken to this gift to higher levels of empowerment. As you open your heart to the possibilities, be prepared to smile.

Chapter 45

Indicator 15 - Increased Spiritual Awareness

Oftentimes your awakening can feel like you are waking up from a dream you've been living in. What you thought was real, no longer feels real. What you once connected with, strangely feels disconnected. What you once thought was important, no longer has any kind of hold over you. What you once thought held power over your life, is now an illusion. Although this seems like some sort of riddle about your life, it isn't any wonder that those in the process of waking up have so many ah ha moments. Your increased awareness has opened up a whole new world of experiences that surpass the mundane routines of the physical world.

A simple analogy of increased awareness is the following. Let's say you've taken the same route to work every day. You pass by the same buildings, the same trees, the same bus stops, the same traffic lights, and intersections, and so on. After a while, the routine of it can get a little mundane to the point that you start to filter out your surroundings. Your mind will often drift to thoughts of other things as you drive and before you know it, you've arrived at work. It happens over and over again.

When you start to wake up to who you are, you will start to see things that you never noticed before on your way to work, like a homeless person who has been on the same corner for the past ten years, yet you never noticed because you got used to the same routine. Now, I am not telling you to take this literally, however, it is a way to explain the experience of increased awareness. Most people go through life in a daze, adopting our roles and our titles, clocking in, and clocking out of work, saving for vacations, a new home, a new car, or the next best gadget. We live in the world presented to us and we think it's pretty normal because that's all we've ever known, that is, until we start to wake up to our internal alarm system. Each of us will experience increased awareness at one time or another and to various degrees depending on our upbringing and our personal experiences with the world.

Increased awareness can be an exciting and positive experience, and also an alarming one. As you begin to open up your seven senses to the world around you, the filters of the physical world gradually come off and it's kind of like seeing what's real for the first time. At first it can be difficult to discern what is real and not real. As you invite increased internal awareness, the external world will have less influence or power over you. In time you may even divorce yourself from everything you thought was supposed to be a part of your life, which can include jobs, people, location, possessions and so on. The value you once place on the temporal things of the world, slowly fade away as you awaken to the things that have eternal spiritual value.

When you are in the process of awakening to increased awareness, your spiritual gifts begin to blossom with great potential. You might unexpectedly discover that you have healing gifts you never even knew existed, or you suddenly feel daring and want to try things you've never considered before.

You've got a whole new world to explore that has promises of love, connection, empathy, compassion, and oneness.

At first you may feel alone, because not everyone you know will be on the same wavelength so to speak, however, in time, you will begin to meet like hearted individuals who are just as excited as you are right now. Your increased spiritual awareness will open up doors of unbelievable opportunities and experiences, as you step into the light of who you are as a divine being. It's kind of like being reborn, seeing life for the first time through the eyes of love consciousness and your connection to everything. Your ability to extend compassion, kindness, empathy, understanding and love will no doubt bless many as your awareness continues to expand into even more awareness.

It is our sincere desire that this material will support you in continued increased spiritual awareness as you learn that your awakening is part of a beautiful grand design created just for you.

Chapter 46

Balancing Increased Spiritual Awareness

Let's face it, learning to create a balanced life can be a juggling act at times and when you begin to become spiritually aware, your whole world can feel like it's been turned upside down. It can be challenging to look at all the things you thought you knew and awaken to a new way of experiencing life. It's definitely a process that does not happen overnight, yet with some simple suggestions, it can make your journey a little less bumpy. The following ideas can support you as you learn to navigate your way to remembering your real identity.

1. Be A Brave and Bold Explorer: Waking up requires you to step out of your comfort zone. As your spiritual awareness increases there will be those that may attempt to hold you back by challenging your new adventurous spirit. Perhaps you've been raised with a particular religion, and you are now stretching the boundaries of those beliefs you've been taught since childhood. Keep in mind that your new spiritual awareness may make others slightly uncomfortable, however, extending understanding, empathy and compassion can go a long way in reassuring your loved ones who may resist the changes. Deep down, those individuals fear abandonment, or some may even feel a sense of betrayal. You may see this temporary resistance

especially with family and close friends. You can reassure and validate concerned individuals by saying things like, "I appreciate your loving concern." Or "Thank you for sharing your thoughts and for caring." Or "I appreciate all you taught me. It has supported me so much in my life." There are many ways you can offer reassurance and validation to help diffuse the energy of resistance. Remember, when you are on a spiritual path of awakening, there is really nothing to defend. You learn to respect all views and continue to move forward into exploring the new you.

2. Be Gentle with Yourself: Leaving old belief systems can feel like you are losing portions of yourself. You are gradually dismantling emotional, mental, spiritual, and physical structures within your adopted belief systems. In a sense this experience can feel like a symbolic death as you release the old you to bring in the new you. There are times as you expand your spiritual awareness that you may look back on choices you've made that may bring up feelings of regret, shame, or self-blame. Your ego may pipe up and say, *"How could you? You should have known better."* We urge you to be gentle with yourself. We'd invite you to look at this newfound spiritual awareness from a different angle.

When a baby is learning to walk, you know that it will fall. There is absolutely no question of that. The baby will get it's bumps and bruises. It will cry when it falls and clap as it masters its first few steps. There is a natural progression of falling and getting back up, and before you know it, the baby is walking with complete wobbly confidence. It's all a part of the journey of mastering something new.

Look at your life. Has it not been like a series of baby steps as you have learned to walk and navigate your way through the obstacles of your mind? Have you not experienced bumps and bruises on various levels from childhood to now? And . . . have you not gotten back up after falling? Have you not fallen in love, vowing to never love again, but yet somehow you found yourself falling in love all over again? The truth is, in the various steps and stages of your life, you have learned to process the art of walking and falling, over and over again. The question is, why would you blame yourself for such a thing? Did it not take courage to get back up each and every time? As you see your life as a series of steps that have led you to where you are right now, think about how amazing that is! How is it that you were led to this very moment? Did you think for one moment that you were alone on that journey of steps? Be gentle with yourself. Treat yourself as you would a baby learning to walk, and before you know it, you'll be moving forward with spiritual confidence.

3. Get Rid of The Weeds: If you hope to ascend to new spiritual awareness, you've got to weed the things out of your life that are choking your spiritual growth. Let's take it to another level with an analogy. Let's say you are wanting to create a new garden filled with beautiful flowers or thriving vegetation. As you look at your garden space, you find that it's filled with old, overgrown weeds from the previous years. It's quite logical that you would want to remove the weeds and cultivate rich soil before planting your new garden, right? So how does this thought have anything to do with spiritual awareness?

When you are cultivating your new spiritual awareness, it's kind of like planting a new garden within the fertile energy of your heart. Your old heart, once connected to the world, may be filled with overgrown weeds of jealousy, envy, bitterness, revenge, and anger. Obviously, you wouldn't think of planting new seeds of growth like love, compassion, understanding, and empathy without first getting rid of the gnarly weeds that tried to take over your heart. You understand that ignoring the old weeds in the garden of your heart and leaving them there, would inevitably choke the life out of the new seeds that are evolving towards thriving and blooming within your new life.

Here's an exercise to support you in preparing your heart for its newly cultivated growth. Draw a heart on a piece of paper. Draw some weeds on the heart and label each weed with an emotional weed that you have felt has taken up residency in your heart's garden. Just write down what comes to you and don't judge it. It could be two emotions or five. Once completed, look at each emotion and determine which emotional weed you are now ready to pull up and out of your heart. It could be regret, or shame, or anger or any other emotion that feels stuck. Next, think of some memories associated with that emotional weed and how it has hindered you from new growth in your life. Just go ahead and take the position of the gardener of your life and observe how you reacted toward the emotional weeds that often revolved around your experiences with people and situations. In this observation, you understand that they no longer have a place in your heart because you know that you can't expect to plant new seeds with the old weeds still present. Now, once you observe the emotional weed you are now ready to pull up and out of your heart, simply rip it away from the page, and toss it in the garbage where it belongs.

This simple and effective exercise can be done over time or in one sitting. A lot of the outcome depends on how quickly you are ready to plant your new garden of joy, love, peace, understanding, empathy, and compassion. The truth is you are the gardener of your heart and you've got some good weeding to do. The more you weed, the more you'll succeed.

"Your heart is a beautiful garden that awaits your presence. As you live your life as the master gardener, you will cultivate new seeds of growth every time you forgive, love, or invite some-one who is homeless . . . into your garden."

- Leslie Paramore

Chapter 47

Indicator 16 - Increased Intuition/ ESP/Telepathy

If you have ever had a gut feeling about something, and discovered that your prediction about something was right, then you have experienced intuition or what we know as glimpses of insight from your third eye chakra. These manifestations can be compared to baby steps in the periodic opening of your third eye. Remember we mentioned briefly that the third eye chakra is connected to the Divine Mind of God, which is also connected to your crown chakra. The reason we state that this particular indicator of intuition is comparable to baby steps in your ascension process is because if your third eye chakra were fully opened, the illusion of the physical world would fade, and the spiritual world would be fully revealed in its complete frequency of divine love. In truth, your physical body would not be able to transition to such a dramatic shift.

Spiritual ascension does not happen overnight. You don't suddenly ascend to a fifth dimensional frequency because you have experienced all of the indicators laid out in this material. As souls, we are given countless opportunities to shift microscopic aspects of our lives and our limited perceptions of self. It's not a race to the finish line as some might believe.

Every soul's progress affects every soul's progress as we are connected on levels that are difficult for the human mind to comprehend. With this you may experience greater intuition, which may include foreseeing events, having visions or powerful spiritual dreams, hearing others' thoughts, or being able to communicate your thoughts to others without physically speaking. Don't be alarmed by these occurrences as these dormant spiritual gifts are now ready to reveal themselves to you.

It can be exciting for new insights to form within, as one may awaken to deeper connections like extra sensory perception which is just a fancy phrase for the keen intuition of the third eye chakra. Also, the ability to communicate on a soul level is referred to as telepathy. Telepathy is a spiritual gift where one can communicate with another merely through the power of heightened spiritual or conscious thought. The person who experiences telepathy has the ability to send thoughts as well as receive and perceive the thoughts of others, without any use or reliance on the awkwardness of physical words or gestures associated with body language.

We could compare the power of telepathy to an invisible frequency wave where the energy of thought travels from the consciousness of one divine mind to another. It's like a sophisticated computer system, communicating in a type of language that is incomprehensible for the human mind to grasp.

In my spiritual experiences which have involved being out of the body, my exchange with spiritual messengers or ascended beings have been unlike any form of communication experienced here on earth. All messages are presented as one complete thought without any movement of the mouth. There really are no words. An analogy to demonstrate what I am explaining would be the following. Human communication through the language of words is fragmented and often misinterpreted, like a puzzle that has not yet been completed, whereas the communication of what I have experienced in the spiritual realms could be compared to a beautiful, flawless picture presented with divine love. That divine love is shared between all with perfect connection and understanding.

The awareness and use of telepathy are a gift afforded to those who are awakening to spiritual ascension. Whatever your first language is, know that it is not actually your first language. Before you came here in physical form, you too spoke in this language of one divine love. In this beautiful place we speak of, there was no division of languages that are very much prevalent on the physical plane.

As a side note, you may or may not have experienced any real consistency with the spiritual gifts of intuition or telepathy, however, be careful not to measure your awakening against such things. Some individuals come with these spiritual gifts activated since birth, while others may need to develop them over time as they learn to connect with the Divine Mind of the I Am consciousness of God. Remember, we are in this together as we remember the truth of our divine inheritance.

"Every soul is born with the divine gift of intuition. It's that spark of infinite light that was poured into your knowing heart, long before your human body took form."

- Leslie Paramore

Chapter 48

Balancing Increased Intuition/ESP/ Telepathy

So here you are feeling as if you have been endowed with some superpowers and you are able to leap over the human mind in a single bound, yet, what do you suppose you were meant to do with this spiritual gift and how can you awaken it to the highest possible use for your soul and the eventual ascension of humanity? The following suggestions can help support you as you navigate your way through expanding your spiritual gifts.

1. Honor & Respect the Gift: When you are endowed with unique spiritual gifts, there is a certain level of responsibility that goes with them. It is important to use your gifts to bless yourself as well as others. Honoring and respecting the spiritual gifts you have acquired will create an energy to expand its uses for the healing of humanity and offering you further insight for your own life as well.

2. Explore Possibilities: Imagine having a gift and never taking the time to use it. If you don't use it, you will most certainly lose it. Even if you have no idea why you may have been

given certain spiritual gifts, you can always explore the possibilities or purpose for that gift. Perhaps your intuitive gift to see through the surface of situations could support you in becoming a counselor. Or perhaps your natural ability to apply intuitive insights regarding the body could lead you into healing work. Having an inquisitive mind and heart may lead you and your gifts to areas in your life that you never even considered. It happened to me, so I most definitely know it can happen to you.

3. Keep Doubt Out of It: Inner doubt can be one of the most powerful inhibitors that can keep you from discovering some of your natural gifts. The power of belief, however, can open up a whole new world of possibilities as you keep your heart open. When spiritual gifts begin to reveal themselves to you, look for ways to expand them by practicing techniques that can support you in that desire. When it comes to spiritual gifts, seeing isn't always believing. Trust that if insights are showing up, that it's an invitation to look a little deeper and to explore the possibilities for your life. Believe to receive.

4. Excuse the Naysayers: During your new adventures in exploring your spiritual gifts, understand that it's your experience and not everyone will resonate with it. For example, if you all of a sudden want to be an intuitive reader with angel cards, and you announce to your friend and family you are leaving your secure job to follow your newfound passion, don't expect everyone to get it. You may meet some opposition along the way; however, I encourage you to listen to the voice within you instead of the voices outside of you. I know a friend who left her job as a gourmet chef at a high-end restaurant to pursue a new calling in her life. She was met with great opposition, especially from her family. They couldn't see the logic of such a huge U-turn in her life, yet she went for it despite

the Nay Sayers. The spiritual calling was so strong that she couldn't ignore it. Today she is a successful spiritual reader and channeler that many seek after for spiritual clarity for their own lives.

As you continue to expand your spiritual gifts, your under-standing of the deep conditioning of the world will broaden. Your ability to be love, show compassion and empathy, and of-fer forgiveness will awaken. You will begin to see through the mortal shell and into the deep heart and soul of humanity. You will begin to understand that your unique gifts were brought to this planet by you, to bless others so that they too may awaken. We ask you to embrace yourself and your gifts and share them with the world. You are so much more than you think you are.

Chapter 49

Indicator 17 - Increased Physical Energy

It only stands to reason that as your spiritual and physical DNA gradually integrate, that you will have increased amounts of energy. Through this supernatural integration, you are being charged by the supporting energy through your divine connection to all that is. Some people refer to this as God, Universal Life Consciousness or Divine Love. In a world conditioned with limitation, it's not surprising that we have a name for this energy, however, no matter what you call it, rest assured you are being supported on multiple levels through your awakening process.

When I was in my twenties, my body required about ten to twelve hours of sleep to feel rested. Even then, I felt tired most of the time due to the conditions in my life at that time, however, as I have been in the process of awakening, my supposed need for sleep has decreased significantly. I have seen myself function perfectly through the day on less than four hours of sleep and still have plenty of energy to accomplish the tasks of my day. I have learned to say, "I've had an adequate amount of sleep."

Perhaps this is now occurring with you. At one time you relied on your physical body to sustain you with energy, by getting plenty of rest, eating food, staying hydrated, or revving
yourself up with caffeinated beverages to get you through
the day. These means are physically based, but what happens
when you have your spiritual circuitry systems lighting you up
with new energy? You have more energy who's supply source
is unlimited!

Initially, as you are learning to adapt to the new levels of
energy and function on less sleep, you may get in your head
about it. You may think that you haven't had enough sleep to
get you through the day, yet we are here to bring to your attention that that is a conditioned head trip you are on. Think
about it. We have been conditioned to think that we need
eight to ten hours of sleep to maintain a healthy and balanced
lifestyle. How can we possibly apply that timetable of sleep for
everyone? The best possible approach that you can take is focusing on the increased energy now available to you, despite
what you might be hearing in the external world. Besides that,
just think about all the money you will be saving not having to
rely so heavily on energy drinks or coffee to get you through
the day. Learning to adapt to the increased energy is all part of
the journey. Take it from someone who has experienced this
shift. Adapting to these new energy levels will level off and
before you know it, you will have adjusted to the change and
those around you will be wondering what you've been doing
with your life to have such great amounts of energy. When you
can understand that these new energy levels are upgrades in
the way of a charge to your body systems, it can be quite exciting to understand what is actually happening to you right now
and within the coming months.

The increased physical energy will serve and bless you on
so many levels. Your body's metabolism will speed up, you will
gain more physical strength and vitality, you will move more

energy blocks that are no longer wanted within your body, and you will have a greater zest for living. Embrace the change. It's been waiting for you.

"There's nothing we need that we don't already have. There's nothing outside of us that is not already within us. There is absolutely nothing flawed, broken or unworthy. There is nothing in this world that can fix, what is already whole."

-Leslie Paramore

Chapter 50

Balancing Increased Physical Energy

One of the most challenging things about having increased energy levels for individuals is wondering what to do with all the excess energy! Now, keep in mind that all this excess energy that has been coming through for you does not take on any sensations of anxiety. The increased energy is actually a good feeling; one that may have you bouncing out of bed at 5:00am while everyone else in your household remains asleep. In efforts to continue to support you through this shift you are feeling, I hope to offer some helpful hints as inspiration comes flowing through for you. Please note and put into action the following suggestions.

1. You've Got to Move It: With all the increased energy you will definitely want to use it for the benefit of your mind, body, and spirit, so I strongly suggest strengthening your physical body through some type of exercise. Now, when some people hear the word, "exercise," they want to run in the other direction because it implies effort and time management. When you find some form of activity that you enjoy doing, it can be incorporated into your daily routine easily. Some suggestions for exercise might be to walk, jog, bike, swim, dance, weightlifting, chi gong, martial arts, participating in a sport, or jump-

ing on a mini trampoline. I personally love to bike early in the morning before my day starts. It's a wonderful way to start my day and give the gift of movement to myself. There are so many possibilities to move your body, mind, and spirit. I would suggest exercising at least three times a week, but for some like me, I much prefer every day. We sleep every day so it only makes sense that we should move our bodies every day for a nice balance between the two.

2. Refrain from Caffeinated Products: When you are going through this increased energy state, the last thing you will need are products that will increase your energy even more so. This heightened energy will be more than enough for you to handle. When you drink caffeinated products, it could lead to excess energy to the point that you begin to feel anxious due to the fact that your system is overloaded, spiritually through the shift and chemically through the beverage. Think of it this way, the gas you use for your vehicle is fuel used to create energy to run your car. If you've got a full gas tank, you're not going to continue trying to fill it right? Your body is no different. If you are being fueled by some supernatural energy, then there's no need in putting more fuel into yourself, as this could potentially create some imbalances, or system overload. Now, I am not saying that the occasional caffeinated drink will hurt you. You know your body better than anyone. Balance everything in moderation and most importantly pay attention to how your body responds if or when you drink caffeinated products. Your excess energy will level off, however, until it does, and until you adjust to it, I would strongly suggest switching your choice of beverages to something like water or decaffeinated drinks.

3. Rest When You Can: Okay this one may seem obvious to some, however, when you have excess energy showing up, un-

derstand that this is what we call a transitional period where your body is adjusting to the physiological shifts, and still requires resting when you can. Resting doesn't necessarily mean sleeping. There were nights where I only rested with no sleep, however, I learned that resting in a meditative state can be beneficial and just as effective as sleep. If possible, I encourage you to rest even midway through the day. Obviously, increased energy levels can be great, however, revving your body's engine too long while adjusting to this shift can create burnout. Some suggestions for resting could be meditating for short periods with conscious breathing, grounding with the earth, taking a hot Epsom salt bath, reading a calming book, or sitting leisurely by a lake. In short keep your life balanced between your increased energy and rest periods. This will go a long way in supporting the energy shifts now taking place within you.

As you experience increased energy levels, you may tune into inspired ideas that will support you through this shift. You are evolving and expanding so many aspects of yourself as your physical and spiritual body work intelligently to merge their energies together, creating a new version of you. Your supernatural shifts are occurring just as they are designed to do as your body increases in its vibrational energy. As always, trust the process and embrace the journey to your progressive ascension.

Chapter 51

Indicator 18 - Vibration or Buzzing Within the Body

I will never forget the very first time that I experienced a buzzing sensation within my body. It was several years ago now. I remember sitting at the computer doing my usual writing when I felt a vibration sensation within my hip area. At first, I thought I had left my phone on vibrate in my pocket, however as I felt down toward my hip, I realized that there was nothing there. I then noticed that my cell phone was conveniently placed on my desk where it normally was.

The only way that I can actually describe this sensation that I am sharing with you is exactly the way I just described. The vibration kind of feels like a cell phone buzzing within your body. You can feel it internally and externally. Initially the sensations are short bursts of vibration that can show up anywhere in the body. When this first happened to me, I had no idea what this strange phenomenon was, however over the years it increased in frequency and duration. Over time this sensation spread throughout my body into a low humming sensation. The interesting thing is, these vibrational sensations began long before I knew anything about healing work, and this phenomenon that we know as ascension or waking up. These shifts were occurring within my physical and spiritual body long before my mind was aware of it. The very fact that this was happening, underscores the intelligences that are working behind the scenes through our period of soul and body integration, destined for ascension.

Often when I conduct an in-person session with clients, I feel this energy flow coursing throughout my body as I channel divine energy for healing. My hands will often heat up as my crown chakra rotates, allowing the energy to filter through and communicate with the client on a mind, body, spirit level. The following day I will check in with a client to see how they are feeling after our session. More often than not, they will remark, I feel a buzzing sensation within my body, or I feel increased energy moving through my body. Now, in many cases, this is often the first time that a client will have experienced such a phenomenon and initially it may be quite alarming to them, however, after explaining that it is merely energy moving through their body, my clients tend to relax. Sometimes I playfully joke and say, *"Welcome to my world,"* meaning, I've been feeling this for years and it's nice to know that others are sharing the same experience.

Perhaps this is happening to you right now. Perhaps you too have found yourself mistakenly reaching for a cell phone that wasn't on your body. Relax. Isn't it a relief to know that you aren't the only one experiencing this? The internal buzzing or vibration is merely your spiritual body activating or communicating with your physical body, lighting up those circuitry systems that we talked about earlier in this material. Through this process, the direct communication between divinely intelligent light frequencies radiating from your soul commune or communicate with the energy pulses of your physical heart. The heart then sends out the information to the body in frequency wave forms that creates the buzzing sensation within your body. It communicates so deeply, that it can be felt right down to the smallest particle in your body. Through this, physical shifts are occurring within DNA structures, and the integration or merging of the physical DNA and spiritual DNA has begun its process, which can in most cases, take years to fully activate itself. For myself, I have been experiencing this for about fifteen or more years now.

Now, keep in mind that some individuals may feel these sensations more strongly than others, and some may have hardly noticed the sensations within their body. In fact, some individuals may be completely oblivious to the vibrations while they sleep, while others may feel periodic sensations throughout the day. The vibrating sensations may come constantly or intermittently, depending on each person. No matter what you may be experiencing or have yet to experience, it is important to trust the process and to relax with the flow of your DNA activation within your body. It's an upgrade that although may feel foreign, is a completely natural part of your evolution as a human being.

Chapter 52

Balancing Vibration
or Buzzing Within
the Body

Now that you have a simple understanding of this foreign vibrating sensation within your body, we'd like to offer some suggestions to support you in living with it, because once it starts, it's not likely to go away. Initially, you may have periods of rest, where a few days or weeks go by without you feeling it, and then suddenly, in the middle of nowhere, and sometimes in the most inconvenient times, the vibrating will start. Trust in the process of receiving it. It is now in motion and has taken on a lifeforce of its own. Some simple things that you can do to accommodate your new experience are the following suggestions.

1. Learn to Laugh About It: As your body creates these changes, be sure to keep lighthearted about it and don't overthink it. Incorporating laughter, instead of overthinking the experience is truly the best medicine for your mind, body, and spirit. When the vibration throughout my body elevated to extreme shaking for eight long months, no doctor could explain what was happening, nor could any medical machine pick up on the divinely orchestrated shifts that were occurring

within me. Now, I am not suggesting that you will experience the same thing, however, I have learned to laugh about such things. This lightens the energy and removes tension from the body.

2. Claim Your Body: Honestly, if there isn't anyone available on the planet to explain what is occurring within you, where do you think you are being invited to look? You are being invited to look inward and to claim ownership over your body. So many individuals give no thought to claiming their body as their own. They take it for granted, misuse it or abuse it. We live in a time where we give greater care to our vehicles than our bodies. When is the last time you gave your body a tune up or fueled it with food or exercise that can help support this process? Understanding what is happening within your body and claiming responsibility for it, is a huge step in your spiritual awakening.

3. Let It Go: Letting go of control invites your spiritual body and physical body to integrate these new energies. Becoming stressed over something you may not understand creates tension in your body which can create energy blockages. Your choice of stress can act like a frequency interrupter for something that is designed to support your ascension process. Let go and let divine intelligence work out the final details.

Chapter 53

Indicator 19 - Rotation of The Chakras

The body consists of seven main energy centers known as the chakras. These beautiful energy wheels can be seen through electromagnetic imaging. In a sense we can say that chakras act like funnels, filtering necessary information for the balanced functioning of your body. Each chakra is connected to certain organ systems within the body, as well as your connection to the heavens and the earth. As you begin your awakening, you may feel these energy centers within the body literally rotating. This is an exciting sensation.

Some may be well acquainted with the chakras, while others may have never heard of them. Whether you know of their existence or not is irrelevant. For the purpose of this material, we will cover the basic functions of your seven chakras within your body. For greater in-depth learning about the chakras, as well as guided meditations to activate your chakras, you can refer to my chakra course on my website, heartcentere-dreiki.org

We will start with the three lower chakras which are associated with your earth experiences. Starting at the base of the spine you have the first chakra or root chakra which is connected to your life's purpose and path and your sense of grounding and connection to the planet. Remember, your root chakra is like the roots of a tree grounding and connecting with everything around you. The second chakra or sacral chakra located just beneath the navel is associated with healthy relationships, friends, life partners, and soulmates. It is connected and associated with your ability to create life and the life around you. The third chakra is the solar plexus chakra, located just below the rib cage. It is associated with your sense of personal power on the physical, emotional, mental, and spiritual levels. Think about the breath of the divine, flowing into your solar plexus chakra every time you inhale and exhale and how that energy can support you in your day to day living.

We've covered the three lower chakras, and now we will look specifically at the heart chakra, or what we will refer to as the bridge between your upper and lower chakras. The fourth chakra is the heart chakra which is your ability to love and also to receive love.

As mentioned earlier, the heart is where the energy of the soul communicates all information to the rest of the body in the form of pulsating waves of divinely intelligent information. The heart chakra can be referred to as the house where the infinite energy of your soul resides. The heart chakra fuels and connects the lower three chakras and also the upper three chakras, bridging the gap between the energies of the earth and the heavens within you. To be clear, the lower three chakras represent the earth energy and the upper three chakras located above the heart, represent the heavens or the universal consciousness of God. In this beautiful reconciliation, taking place within the energy field of the heart chakra, the heavens, and the earth within you, seek to meet.

Remember the buzzing sensations we discussed earlier? It's all coming together now as we explain the process further. The energy of the heart chakra communicates with all other chakras, channeling divine energy that is filled with information necessary for the ascension process. Each chakra is then activated according to its ability to receive and process the information. The rotations of the chakras, both clockwise and counterclockwise then proceed to send out the information to the physical body, for spiritual and physical integration.

At this time, we feel it would be beneficial to bring in some information for you concerning the rotation of the chakras to bring further clarity and understanding. There is a common goal in the spiritual community that it is a good thing to have your chakras opened and not closed. While this is partially true, we wish to bring you further clarification. It is neither beneficial to have your chakras completely open all the time or completely closed all the time. The clockwise and counterclockwise rotations of the chakras are in constant motion depending on the life experiences and choices of an individual. Each rotation, both clockwise and counterclockwise has a specific function within the body.

When the heart chakra has its circuitry systems activated through your connection with the universal consciousness of God, it then sends information to the chakras that are open to receiving it. This is why meditation can be helpful, for in that stillness, void of all distractions, it opens the crown chakra to filter through the energy needed to activate the whole process. When the divine energy is filtered through the crown chakra, and gathered in the heart chakra, the heart chakra then begins to energetically filter the information to all other chakras. The signal waves of the heart chakra cause the intended chakras to rotate clockwise expanding their energy fields, in preparation to receive the channeled energy. We could call this beautiful energy manna from heaven, or even the breath of God, which is designed to nourish all parts of our being. As the information is processed, the chakras then rotate counterclockwise, condensing the energy and locking in the information to a more condensed frequency that the physical body can integrate more easily and effectively. Once this process is done, the energy can then be channeled to the physical organ systems of the body, providing necessary and sustainable energy.

Now that you have a greater visual of how the heart chakra orchestrates the conduction of divine energy, we will now move on to the upper three chakras which represent the universal consciousness of God or what I refer to as divine love in its fullness.

The chakra just above the heart chakra is the fifth chakra or the throat chakra, which is the chakra of expression and your ability to speak your truth. Your words hold the power of creation and also send out a vibration much like the heart chakra. The difference is, your voice sends out energy waves of information and manifestations to the physical world, whereas your heart sends out divine energy to your internal world. Let's continue with the sixth chakra, which is the third eye chakra located in the middle portion of your brow. In the mentioning of this before we identified it as being connected to the divine mind of God. The third eye chakra is the chakra responsible for of clarity, focus, concentration, intuition, and spiritual intelligence. Finally, we note the significance of the seventh chakra is the crown chakra located at the top of your head which is connected to universal consciousness. When you were an infant, the portal of the crown chakra was open in the area known as, the soft spot. There we can physically witness the communication of the divine connecting with the heart as the energy pulse of the heart, located on the soft spot, can be seen with the naked eye. Perhaps this is something you have never even considered, and now we bring it to you for deep consideration. As a baby grows, the soft spot slowly closes over, yet the energy of the portal is still there. You too had a soft spot as an infant that also closed over, yet the energy of the portal is still there. Take a moment to focus on that area through meditation and deep breathing. As you do so, you may feel a tingling or rotating sensation. It is responsible for receiving direct communication from the universal realms.

Now that we have covered the basics of the seven chakras, we hope that you have obtained a deeper understanding of just what an important role they play in your body systems and your ascension process. The rotating sensations are real and definitely not a figment of your imagination.

The very first time I felt a chakra rotating was when I attended a group meditation revolving around the energy of sound. There were Tibetan bowls, flutes, and chimes, among a few other instruments to invoke a sense of peace and calm. During a part of the meditation, a flute was played and magically, without any warning, my third eye chakra began to rotate. Now for those of you who may have never experienced this sensation before, you might wonder what that felt like. The best way to describe my personal experience was that I felt a warm tingling sensation rotating on my skin that felt like it was coming and expanding from inside of me. It is still fascinating to me when the rotation sensations of my chakras occur at any given moment. Now that I understand what is actually happening, it brings a smile to my face.

As you feel your chakras rotating you may feel a similar sensation, yet everyone processes these sensations differently. Just know that the heist version of yourself is working hard behind the scenes to bring all of your chakras in alignment with the universal consciousness of God, and also, in preparation for reconciliation and communion at the heart.

Chapter 54

Balancing Rotation of The Chakras

Now that you have a new awareness of what is actually happening with your chakras, you may be wondering what you can do to support the process of creating vibrational alignment within them. The following suggestions can be helpful as you implement them on a consistent basis.

1. Feel What's Real to Heal: One of the greatest things you can do, is to feel the sensations within your body. This can be physically, emotionally, mentally, and spiritually as you tune into your chakras. When the vibration begins, when possible, take a few minutes to visualize your chakra being imprinted with energy that is going to help benefit your chakras as well as your organ systems. Feel the sensation and receive the energy being channeled specifically for you. For example, what emotion comes up as you feel the energy surface? Are you feeling excited, nervous, uncertain? What does the sensation feel like physically? Is it a light tingling sensation or is it a heavy sensation that feels like it is being cleared? Tune into the directional sensation that is occurring within the chakra. Is it rotating clockwise or counterclockwise? How are you feeling mentally? You get the idea. Feel to heal.

2. Listen to Guided Chakra Meditations: It can be helpful to listen to guided meditations specifically created to support your chakras. I personally have several guided meditations for the chakras that you can tune into on You Tube. A guided meditation will energetically guide you through certain shifts and work with all aspects of you. Tune into the meditations that seem to resonate with you. You'll know it is in resonance with your body, mind, and spirit when you feel peaceful and re-laxed. Do what works for you. If you find a meditation that res-onates with you, stick with listening to it and allow it to work harmoniously with your chakras. You can listen to a guided meditation several times a week and benefit from it.

3. Pay Attention to Your Life: There are things that you can do to support your chakras as you live your life in abundant ways. As you become familiar with each chakra and its func-tion, you will definitely want to empower that chakra by living in alignment with it. For instance, if you are looking to expand your emotional and mental state associated with your root chakra, you may need to work through fears around survival, security, and your sense of safety. With these energy block-ages removed, you can move from merely surviving to thriving. In addition, in order to support yourself and your chakras, you will want to pay attention to the thoughts that you are sending to your body as well as your words that you are speaking into your life and also the actions that you take toward the next steps of your life. When your thoughts, words and actions are congruent with one another, or in other words, in agreement with the same focused intention, your life will begin to shift in huge and miraculous ways.

4. Receive a Reiki / Chakra Balancing Session: One of the ways you can help support the energy systems of your chakras is to receive an energy balancing session where a Reiki practi-

tioner will channel direct energy to your chakras, clearing away stagnant energy that can interfere with the receptivity, connection and alignment of your chakras. In private sessions, I have seen so many individuals who are weighed down with a sense of heaviness, come for a clearing. Once completed they walk away feeling so much lighter with a visible shift in their countenance. Some clients have even looked in the mirror and after seeing and feeling a difference, have broken down crying.

Although you cannot physically see the chakras rotating clockwise and counterclockwise, this is a very real part of you. They are energy batteries filled with information to support you throughout your life. It is exciting to know that you can help support their growth and expansion just by learning about them and implementing new practices into your life. I am sure there are other ways of supporting your chakras that you will discover in time. For now, work on these few suggestions, all designed to support your mind, body, spirit, and let's not forget . . . your chakras.

Chapter 55

Indicator 20 - Vivid Spiritual Dreams or Visions

Dreams can have many meanings which can hold symbolic significance within our lives as we step into examining the types of dreams that are being created subconsciously. Some dreams can seem like a scrambled puzzle making no sense at all, with convoluted images that seem energetically distorted and disconnected. Some dreams can take a dark turn, invoking hyped up adrenaline to course through bodies, forcing some to bolt upright from their beds. Some dreams are filled with past memories of pain being worked out through subconscious minds, or on the other hand, some dreams can project individuals into the future of the unknown. Dreams are filled with symbolism and messages that can invoke all kinds of emotions, reactions, and interpretations. Even if you think you don't dream, you do . . . for life is a dream and you are simply waking up from it.

As we speak of visions and dreams as one of the ascension indicators, we can't forget to mention those dreams that somehow feel different from all other dreams. It's like they have a rite of passage into the unknown realms of the spirit world. The dreams we speak of are most often referred to as supernatural. These dreams can be filled with peaceful experiences. One may find themselves being visited by heavenly messengers often surrounded by illuminating light, conveying messages of truth. Such dreams can also give individuals glimpses into their futures with insights unknown to the mind or heart of the mortal man. They can also offer pertinent information concerning spiritual identity, guiding the experiencer in remembering their path and their purpose in both the spiritual and physical realms of reality. There may be times when one of these unique dreams manifest as an outer body experience as the individual moves beyond the experience of their current physical perceptions of reality. Many have had such dreams that we speak of.

As one of the possible indicators for awakening to ascension, we speak of dreams and visions not to sensationalize the ascension process, but to note that this tends to be an occurrence that is rare, however, still possible. Not all will experience such supernatural things, however, this does not take away from their own awakening. The human mind may reason that if an individual has had such dreams or visions that there must be something uniquely special about them. The truth is every soul is special and are on their own trajectory and timeline to experience such things.

Perhaps you have experienced supernatural, dreams, visions, or visitations with heavenly beings. If this is the case, we encourage you to take notes and be prepared to take the information offered to bless humanity to the fullest degree. Often those who experience visions and dreams are what we refer to as spiritual messengers. Most times they may not recognize themselves as such as they are too attached to their titles and identities of the physical world. It is often through the awakening process that individuals discover that they came to do something beyond what their current life dictates.

Imagine going to school, getting a degree, and then not using those newly acquired skills to bless the lives of yourself and others. What would be the purpose in that? Ignoring the dreams or visions that have come into your life for a reason is the equivalent of ignoring your spiritual calling in life. In a sense, I suppose we could say that you are being taught in a spiritual school designed to prepare you for greater things than you ever thought possible.

If you are one who has experienced any spiritual phenomenon, consider yourself destined to become a spiritual messenger. Now, keep in mind that nothing will ever be forced upon you. This is a choice you can make in this life, or perhaps in another life. Even if you think you could not do such a thing, you will eventually. The role of spiritual messenger may indeed be a part of your souls' spiritual mastery to accomplish. It is a role of great responsibility and discipline and definitely not for the faint of heart. We encourage you to embrace the spiritual shaping of your soul and learn from the masters who also have a role in conveying important messages to you.

Chapter 56

Balancing Vivid Spiritual Dreams or Visions

To be the recipient of spiritual dreams and visions can be a beautiful experience, yet it can also be overwhelming if not balanced. The following suggestions can support you in maintaining a healthy flow revolving around the messages that are coming in for you or will be coming through to you in divine timing. These suggestions can also help those who would like to experience these types of connections with the spiritual realms.

1. Be Open with Reception and Intention: A person's receptivity and intention can go a long way in experiencing unique relationships with the spiritual realms. Some of you may be aware of the scriptural verse, "Knock and the door will be opened. Seek and ye shall find. Ask and it shall be given." Your desires and intentions are never left unheard, yet it can seem that way at times. In order to connect with this desire to experience dreams, visions or even visitations, there must be a consistent energy manifested through your thoughts, words, and actions. In other words, your consistent communication through meditation, prayer and daily intention can help create

positive results. In order to connect with the frequency of the spiritual realms, you must live in the frequency of love, compassion, empathy, kindness, and the ways of divine truth.

2. Believe to Receive: The most common thing that can get in the way of a person connecting with the spiritual realms is the energy of doubt. Doubt creates an energy field around a person that can block receptivity and connectivity. Typically, what happens in this world is an individual may wish they could experience a dream, vision, or connect with the angelic realms; however, they may simply wish, not ever believing that it can happen for them. This blockage is typically attached to the emotion of feeling unworthy to experience such a divine gift. The first step is believing that such beautiful experiences do occur, and the second step is opening your heart up to receive. Imagine the possibilities if you could believe right now that a dream is waiting to be realized right into your reality.

3. Imagine Dreams into Reality: Everything that ever came to be manifested was first created within the realms of the imagination. To create the energy to expand your connections with the spiritual realms you can begin by imagining it occurring right now. You do not have to wait for the dream state to begin to experience the beginnings of something beautiful. An exercise for you to begin manifesting dreams and visions right now is to simply step into a daydream of your very own creation and see it occurring naturally. Allow your senses to come into the vision. Bring in the sights, sounds, colors, and other sensations into view. See it right in front of you in a panoramic view and be clear on the intentions set. In a sense, it may seem unlikely that this would strike the flame for spiritual visitations, however, your actions are like a prayer created within the realms of your heart. Practice seeing the possibilities, then one day without warning, you may find yourself slipping into

an out of body experience that will grow beyond your wildest imagination.

4. Expect the Unexpected: Sometimes we can get caught up in what we think is supposed to happen with what we refer to as spiritual phenomenon. Not every spiritual experience shows up the same way for everyone. Often in my outer body experiences I have encountered heavenly messengers that stand in a luminous white light that appears to be alive with loving intelligence. In recent years, I have encountered this same light within my physical surroundings in my healing rooms. It was totally unexpected, yet there it was, as plain as day. Was this some type of trickery that my mind was playing on me? No matter how much I rubbed my eyes, it wasn't going away. It has appeared many times with witnesses to attest that it was in fact there. The spiritual realms will always communicate on levels that we can comprehend and process. Expect the unexpected by not limiting yourself to what those encounters can look like.

5. Build Momentum with Gratitude: It is indeed a privilege to connect with the spiritual realms. Through this much can be graciously granted through their instruction, counsel, healing, and loving intentions. The pure expression of gratitude can awaken the vibration of the heart to beautiful visitations unknown to the human mind, yet open to the desires of a willing heart. Express gratitude even before you experience the gift of divine presence in your life, for most are not even aware that divine presence is always with us. Express gratitude for the workings of spirit. In doing so, you foster the energy of communion and communication in ways that will bless you long after your experiences have passed. Your dreams are now waiting for your awakening.

Chapter 57

Indicator 21 - Feeling Deep Connections of One

We live in a time where life may be appearing as a huge unsolvable puzzle scattered carelessly throughout the world. With evidence of various levels of division, it can seem insurmountable as we witness how humans react to humans, or how humans tend to solve problems. It can seem like one big mystery that becomes more perplexing as time goes on.

As you move into deeper and deeper awareness through your awakening, you will begin to have profound experiences and insights as you feel greater connections with those around you. You will begin to understand the intricate web of intelligence that weaves each of us together. Our thoughts, words, and actions, create cascading energy that ripples outward to all, excluding no one regardless of where they may be in the world, what their belief systems are, what cultures they are immersed in, or what race or gender they are. As we connect on deeper levels, we understand that everyone on this beautiful planet is part of a greater whole called, One.

One of the first times I experienced this thing we call becoming One was when I went to an event where I met another person attending as well. This person was so familiar to me as we talked and exchanged thoughts with each other. It was quite a peculiar situation as I had never experienced an encounter quite like this one. The conversation and energy exchanged was so connecting that I literally saw and felt that she was a part of me. I saw another version of myself in her eyes. Toward the end of the conversation she remarked, *"You look and feel so familiar to me."* Surprisingly, without thinking, I calmly stated, "I know what you mean. I see myself in your eyes. We are connected on deeper levels than what may be apparent here."

It is a beautiful thing when you capture moments like that. Experiencing a glimpse of what oneness can feel like and be like, is something that all of us will eventually discover within themselves. Do you remember that saying that our parents or someone else may have said to bring us down a notch or two? *"The world does not revolve around you."* BUT . . . what if it did? What if the world did revolve around you? What if everything you are experiencing externally, are reflections of unhealed wounds that you have within yourself? What if your internal healing and self-acceptance could reflect love throughout the world to create deliberate shifts for higher consciousness? What if you were that powerful? What if there was no more room for blaming what others have done to you? What if you just stepped up and proclaimed, "On some higher level, I created everything I have experienced through and through?"

When you are one with yourself, meaning no longer divided within yourself, I think you will find that your external experiences will shift. You will no longer look at a beggar the same way, for you will miraculously see them as a part of yourself that begs not for money, but for love, acceptance, compassion, empathy and understanding. One of the things I like to do to practice this idea of oneness, is this. As I come upon an experience, I will observe it, then I will ask the question, "If that person were me, how would I like to be served or honored?

How would I respond lovingly to myself?" When this question is asked, there are so many opportunities that can be unveiled before our eyes to create the energy of oneness and divine connection. One such experience I am feeling impressed to share.

I was out and about running my usual errands when I suddenly felt an abrupt distraction from my stomach. I have gotten so caught up in my errands, I had forgotten to eat. I asked my body, *"What sounds good right now?"* And I immediately got feedback in the form of an intuitive impression, *"A green smoothie."* Luckily for me, I was in the area of a well-known smoothie place. As I ordered the smoothie, I noticed an old man in a wheelchair, barely able to stand, hunched over to get a drink of water. Without expecting it, I hear that internal voice, *"Get him one too."* It was a hot day so without any hesitation, I ordered two green smoothies, one for me and one for my new friend. I drove into the parking lot close to where that man was sitting on the curb with his sign. More than anything I had this instant desire to bless him that day. I thought, *"I'll give him the smoothie and a five-dollar bill."* The passing thought was overridden by a higher portion of myself. *"Give him everything you have in your wallet."* Okay, I'm going to be brutally honest here. I had no idea how much money I had in my purse. I only saw a wad of it conveniently tucked into my wallet as I had paid for the smoothies. I hesitated, then the inner voice said, *"Are you going to miss it? Are you going to miss that money if you give it to him?"* Of course, the answer was, *"No."*

I couldn't help but count the money to see how much I was giving up. That's what my mind told me, however, my heart told me otherwise. The gift was definitely going to bless him, however, by the simple act of doing so, it would bless me as well.

I went over and tapped him on the shoulder. As he turned around, I was greeted with a huge smile and a warm hello. I promptly passed him the drink before making any formal introductions and said, *"I thought you might enjoy a cold drink on such a hot day."* He thanked me immediately and then without me asking, he began to share his story of how he ended up where he was. He was a war veteran, and it appeared like life had handed him a raw deal. I could feel his shame, humiliation, regrets and lowliness as he seemed to drown helplessly in his own words. I gently placed my hand on his shoulder and said, *"You don't have to explain to me how you got here. It's okay. I just wanted to bless you today."* He seemed relieved at my comment. I then clumsily dug into my purse and grasped the money that was meant for him that day. I passed it to him. He looked down and his eyes got wide with tears. He stuttered and stammered, now tripping over his words of astonishment. *"Thank you. You have no idea. I can't believe this. Thank you. I don't know what to say."* I smiled, and once again placed my hand on his shoulder. *"I just wanted to bless you today."* I walked toward my car smiling in my heart. I felt elated and blessed at such an opportunity to bless another. As I drove away, I watched him as he sat energetically elevated in his wheelchair. The oneness I felt at that moment of connection is one that will be with me for a very long time.

The truth is, on a deeper level, we are all remembering that essence of oneness and connection. As each of us moves into the oneness within, the lines of division will fade between cultures, religion, race, gender, creed and humanities insecurities of separateness. Perhaps we have a great opportunity during these times to attend to humanity in ways that will foster that sense of oneness. We are all one body struggling to come back together again. What part will you be? Will you be the heart of the world; the heart that blesses all you encounter? The heart that sees know division within the hearts of humanity.

"The beat of your heart creates a symphony of sounds as you experience life on every conceivable level. Live boldly, holding nothing back, for in doing so the song of your life will be heard and experinced by all."

\- Leslie Paramore

Chapter 58

Balancing Feeling Deep Connections of One

Becoming one with all may seem like an impossible thing to realize, however, let's begin this process with you and you, alone. Let's create ways within you to support this idea of the kind of oneness that defies all the logic of the human mind and elevates it to the divine heart. The following suggestions are given to support you in this process of awakening.

1. Be an Instrument of Love Consciousness: What better way to begin your day than to have the intention of being an instrument of love in action? Imagine waking up with the pure intent to bless someone's life that day. You can start off small like smiling at a stranger or opening the door for someone. As you get comfortable, you can expand your love by stepping into bigger forms of action like bringing someone dinner, visiting a loved one who has been ill, or leaving encouraging notes on people's cars. Think about all the fun you could have as your creative mind and heart sit in the driver's seat of possibilities. Imagine surprising people with unexpected blessings and how that could turn around to bless you.

2. Stare if You Dare: Do you remember having staring contests when you were a child? The object of the game was to stare into someone else's eyes without looking away or blinking. We know that generally, most people avoid eye contact because it may feel slightly uncomfortable. We can see this all around us. Look at how people stand on an elevator, staring forward and pretending that those around them are not even there. All the missed opportunities for connection go down with the elevator with them. Now, in this simple exercise, we are not asking you to stare deeply into a stranger's eyes, however, we are suggesting that you make a point of having eye contact with people you encounter throughout the day. For instance, if you are walking by someone who is traveling in the opposite direction of you, make eye contact and say a warm hello. They may try to avoid it, but that's okay, do it anyway. If you are opening the door for someone, smile and make eye contact. I promise it will get easier as you go. Pretty soon, you'll be so comfortable with it you will see those you encounter as an old friend you are simply remembering as you commit to making eye contact.

3. Be Aware of The Dividing Line: This exercise will bring you back to your school days, however, it will be used to support you in becoming more aware of the division that you may be experiencing within yourself. In this exercise, simply draw a picture of yourself. Don't worry, you don't have to be an artist to do this. If need be, a simple stick figure will do just fine. After you have drawn the picture of yourself, add to your creation by drawing a mind, and then a heart. Once you have a picture of yourself, with a mind and a heart, the next step is to draw a horizontal line between the mind and the heart which will visually divide the two. Here's where the fun begins. Think of some things in your life that tends to divide your mind and your heart. A clue on how to tune into this, is to

think of things that you have mixed feelings about. Here's an example. Someone asks you to go to a party, yet you've outgrown the party scene and prefer the solitude of meditation. Out of feelings of obligation, you skip the meditation and go to the party. The reason we are suggesting doing this is to bring in the awareness of possible ways that could be hindering you from creating oneness within yourself. It's a great exercise to do daily. Are you conflicted? Write that down!

4. Visualize What You Feel: Visualization is a powerful tool to create a positive energy around you, especially when you feel the emotion that is connected to it. Since you are feeling great desires to become one with all, see it happening and also feel the emotion of that experience. The charged emotions of your heart are powerfully connected to your divine mind that can foresee the future possibilities of oneness. Feel like it would be like to surround yourself with like-heart and like-minded individuals and how beautiful that would be. Now we are not saying that people are going to flock to you instantaneously, however, it will happen gradually as you imagine it happening through the connection of your mind and heart.

5. Be Present to Be One: It's kind of difficult to have connections of oneness with all if you are somewhere other than in the present moment. In other words, if your mind is drifting to past experiences that are charged with negativity, you automatically disconnect yourself from the beautiful opportunities all around you because you have placed your energy somewhere else. Also, if you have projected yourself into the future, dreaming of what could be, you are not present in the moment, because you have placed your energy on a future event which may or may not even be real. To be in the present moment, means exactly, right now. What is happening right now? What picture can you create with all of your seven senses fully en-

gaged and alive? What are you aware of as you see that picture? It is a common scientific fact that we tend to filter out so much of our experiences and that only a fraction of it can be processed, however, we are suggesting that when you are truly present, a whole new world will be unveiled, not only in the physical world, but also within the unseen worlds of the spiritual realms. You will understand your divine connection to absolutely everything.

Allow us to offer an example of a simple connection. Imagine a fly buzzing around you in the house. What would you do? Most people would reach for the closest fly swatter and kill it. Now, I used to kill flies and thought nothing of it. I mean, isn't that why fly swatters were made, so we can take our repressed anger out on the flies, who accidently found their way into our house? What I'm about to share with you could potentially change the way you look at flies.

So, you might be wondering how you can be present with a fly. At first mention of being present with a fly, it may seem totally ridiculous, yet I would suggest that if you can be present with a fly, you can be present with anything. Your energy is more powerful than you know. The way you move your body, the thoughts that you think and project, the words you speak, and even the beat of your heart, ripple out energy that you aren't even conscious of. Now . . . let's get back to the fly.

I like to put things to the test. I mean, if I am teaching concepts, it would only make sense that I would test them out myself. One late evening, there was a fly buzzing around in my kitchen. This fly had taken up residency in my house for a period of three days and quite frankly I was ready to evict the fly for disturbing the peace. The question was, how could I get the fly out of my house without killing it? With a flash of insight. I had an unexpected thought, "If everything is energy and we are constantly sending out energy waves, then this fly should be able to feel that energy as well." In short, I should be able to communicate with the fly through the frequency of thought and intention.

I intuitively felt impressed to get a spoon and I placed the spoon on the counter as I continued to hold the end of it to support it. Now, here's where we step outside of the box of ordinary thinking, so bear with me. With a specific intention of energy, I sent out a frequency of love consciousness, radiating from myself to the spoon and then to the fly. Surprisingly, within a few short seconds, the fly walked across the counter and climbed onto the spoon. I was completely astonished. I carefully walked across the kitchen floor, opened the sliding glass door, and extended my arm outside. The fly flew off and my experiment had been completed. *Coincidental?* I thought. After that one experience I have since been successful in repeating it over and over again. Releasing fly after fly to the great outdoors, on a spoon. Give it a try to see how you fly!

I share this story, to make a point. You can literally become one with everything in ways that energetically connect and communicate through higher levels of love and empathy. In the meantime, there are opportunities waiting to be explored and discovered all around you. There are many ways that you can create feelings of oneness, first within yourself and then that energy will ripple outward to others. Change will occur, one heart at a time as we ascend to oneness together

Chapter 59

Living in The Moment of Now

So here we are having navigated our way through the 21 Signs of spiritual awakening, designed to move you forward toward your timely ascension. Perhaps in this material presented, you were able to identify or relate with several of the indicators or maybe just a few. Nonetheless, as mentioned earlier, whatever your current experience may be, it's showing up for the benefit of your personal spiritual awareness and the multiple levels of your soul's expression and expansion.

The moment of now has come where you are learning to harness the energy that is available to you right now. In true reality, what other time is there than right now? This moment of connection, this moment of thought, this moment of words, this moment of action. The only way to successfully navigate your way through this moment is right now. Let's share a simple analogy to prove a point.

Imagine yourself as the captain of a sailboat, and it's your intention to get from point A to point B in a certain period of time. Obviously, as you begin your journey, you would need to be very conscious of the depth of the water, the changing tides, the winds, and the direction of your course. You place focus as your rutter, and trust as your sail, and gratitude as your vessel. Imagine what would happen, if you started to daydream as you are sailing your boat, thinking back to the past when you first started your journey. Perhaps thoughts of storms you had gone through arise, or perhaps you find yourself thinking of times when you were stuck, which left you feeling anchored in experiences that felt out of your control. You get swept away by thinking about the past, which then invites that energy right to where you are in your current situation as you are navigating your sailboat. You realize that you have lost your focus and have gone off course. Our point is, placing your time and energy in the past, robs you of your powerful moment of right now, and also keeps you from moving forward in life, in the direction you are setting. The same can happen when you place your attention of the future which hasn't even occurred, yet your projections of worry or concern, can also rob you of what you have right in front of you. To harness the energy of right now, is really the only time available to you. Everything else is a waste of time; not to mention your energy.

The reason we wish to emphasize this moment of right now, is because this is the most powerful position that you can be in to navigate your life in the direction that you wish to go right now. If you find yourself drifting to the past which is now over, or to the future which hasn't even arrived, it can drain you of the energy you need to work through the indicators that you may be experiencing currently. Your focus of intention is what matters right now.

Let's talk briefly about your focus. If you are one who seems to be experiencing a few of these indicators, you may be feeling overwhelmed. A way to balance these feelings is to observe and prioritize. You can begin by asking yourself, which indicator seems to be more prevalent in your life? Which one is staring you right in the face? Chances are, it is that indicator that needs the most attention right now. Here's an exercise for you to do to help prioritize the indicators which may be showing up.

1. Make a Personal List: Make a list of the 21 indicators so that you have them right in front of you. View the list. As you view the list, you may find that there may be indicators that you have already experienced and brought into balance. There may be indicators that you have not yet experienced, and there may be indicators that you are currently experiencing. As you go through the list, first circle the indicators that you have not yet experienced and set them aside from your thoughts for now. Once you've completed that step, next, put a line through those indicators that you feel that you have managed to successfully navigate your way through that no longer needs your attention. And finally, place a checkmark by the indicators that you are currently experiencing. What we are doing through this exercise is supporting you in prioritizing your life, outlining which indicators now need your attention to help move you forward.

2. Establish the Relevance: Now that you have the indicators highlighted that need your attention, write them on a separate piece of paper. Once you have them written down, we would like you to look at the list to determine which ones are most relevant in your life right now to the least relevant in your life. Write down the list again, this time placing the most relevant at the top of the list to the least relevant at the bottom of the list. Perhaps you have seven things on your list or three indicators on your list. What matters is the order you've placed them in.

3. Prioritize Your List: When we talk about priorities, we can have a clear understanding of what needs our immediate attention right now. As you look at the indicator at the top of

the list that would be your very first priority to address. For instance, let's say you are transitioning to a new job and that is at the top of your list. It would only make sense that that would come before another indicator like changes in belief systems. Although you may be experiencing both at once and you really enjoy exploring your new beliefs, be sure to keep things in balance so you are not losing sight of the things that will keep you grounded in creating the best possible life for yourself.

4. Note the Connection: Some indicators may be worked on together as they complement one another. For instance, perhaps you are currently experiencing changes in belief systems which has led you to the art of meditation. You can use meditation to find the perfect job for you as you tune into your keen intuition. Use your intuition with respect to which indicators could go hand in hand and complement each other.

5. Be an Action Figure: Once you have established which indicator is a priority, be sure to implement some of the suggestions offered in this material, or perhaps some ideas of your own that can help support you in bringing them into balance. Remember, baby steps work best, and consistency is key in creating the best results for your brand-new life.

Living in the now moment will afford you ample time and energy as you ascend to your spiritual awakening on multiple levels. If you find yourself drifting toward past events or anticipating future events, take a deep breath and pause. Bring yourself back to right now, the moment that has been here all along, right in the center of your heart. Your soul knows exactly how to navigate its way into your heart and the merging of the two will undoubtedly lift you to new spiritual awareness's that are preparing you for your timely ascension.

Chapter 60

Embracing the Paradigm Shift

Let's get real here. We all have days where challenges can sometimes rob us of seeing through the veil of our body, yet what a beautiful thing that rest can afford us. In the evening we lay our bodies down, and retire from the happenings of the day, opening ourselves up to rest, reprieve, and reflection. The sunsets of our lives, offer the perfect chance to resurrect any previous thoughts, words, or actions that may not have been in harmony with our highest selves. As we sleep, there are no doubt beautiful beings of light supporting each of us in resurrecting every aspect of ourselves, mind, body, and spirit. I personally will ask with a prayer of pure intent that those invested in my life, dwelling in the spirit world would send healing to my body, mind, and spirit. I embrace any healing that will elevate my heart to a new level of awareness. I might suggest that you do the same. Often as we sleep, we tend to be more restful and open to receiving the blessings awaiting us.

The birthing of the new you, is most certainly a daily process. Every day you wake up to the newfound possibilities for your abundant life. Think of every morning as a resurrection of sorts. It can be like seeing life for the first time. Every sunrise asks you to now rise to your ascension, one step at a time, one word at a time, one thought at a time, and one action at a time. It's like a synchronized dance between our divine heart and mind.

What are you willing to embrace right now? There is most definitely a shift occurring individually and collectively. If you are still unsure about this, let me ask you something. "Are you the same person today that you were five years ago? Have you not grown in awareness in one way or another?" I think most would answer that they have experienced shifts or changes within themselves that have manifested through their life's unique experiences. Sometimes these shifts can be met with relative ease, while other times they take a more concerted effort, as you have probably discovered. No matter what, it is how we choose to meet these shifts that matters. Such choices can determine how quickly we resurrect to our spiritual ascension.

Now remember that the way you choose to greet each day, not only affects you, but also creates a ripple effect that affects others in ways that we may never know fully, and this is why I have made it a habit to embrace each day with gratitude, for each day is a sacred gift offered to each of us. I have found when we are able to have an open heart and an open mind that life tends to go smoother, as it requires us to move into a deeper trust in recognizing that we are not alone on this journey.

The material presented here is yours to process. As mentioned earlier, embrace what resonates with you and put it to good and effective use by applying the knowledge and suggestions laid out especially for you. I encourage you to go over the material often, so that it can continue to support you through the various twists and turns of life.

This is my gift to you. A labor of love from the most authentic parts of myself. I pray you will be blessed as you embrace the paradigm shifts that are happening externally and internally. I am here for you personally, and I extend an invitation for you to personally contact me with any questions or concerns you might have. Simply reach out to *leslie@heart-centered-productions.com* and will be so pleased to hear from you. I'd also be interested to hear about your ascension indicators and how you are working through them. I have a strong belief that we are better together. May you be blessed. May you be love. May you ascend to the greatness already within you.

"Every sunrise offers you a priceless gift - the chance to breathe, to be, and to believe in yourself. You are the greatest creative expression of a miracle that ever was, however, in order to realize that miracle unfolding, you must first believe in you."

- Leslie Paramore

Chapter 61

Dismissing The Labels

Words are powerful and their power literally becomes a part of our own creations, through our quiet thoughts, through our spoken words, and through our deliberate actions. The irony about my personal relationship with words has quite a twist. In the very beginning of my school years, I was the most unlikely to succeed with the written word. I struggled to read and was placed in the lowest reading group in first grade called, *"The Purple Turtle."* It was like a stamp of failure to my child's mind. *"I was doomed from the start,"* At least that's what I thought as a child. I worked really hard to be like everyone else in my class; proficient at reading. I didn't understand how words came so easily to them, and I, a very shy child, struggled to even speak them out loud.

I have often found that as we remove the limiting labels that others have given us, and the labels we have given ourselves, we are given the freedom to expand our own internal awareness's about ourselves. No matter where you are in life, no matter where you've been, no matter how you perceive yourself, each day invites an opportunity to shift into more conscious versions of yourself. By choosing to remove the labels, you are invited to step into accountability for you life and the direction it is now going.

Today, I hold onto a reminder that labels and titles are not true, and should never ever have the power to define us.

"Not too well adjusted to her grade level. Seldom answers a question orally. Quite shy and never makes a decision. A very quiet child, but she's trying to do her best." - Mrs. Ashford.

THE WENTWORTH COUNTY BOARD OF EDUCATION   L. R. MUMFORD
Director of Education

INTERIM APPRAISAL REPORT

PUPIL *Leslie Duncan*   SCHOOL *Queens Rangers*

GRADE, UNIT OR LEVEL *2*   PHONE *627-7829*

DATE *Oct 29, 1971*

Not too well adjusted to her grade level. Seldom answers a question orally. Quite shy and never makes a decision. A very quiet child; but she is trying to do her best.

PRINCIPAL *McGovern*   TEACHER *M. Ashford*

Perhaps you too were labeled as a child, and perhaps those labels have influenced the way you have made your decisions in life, yet just like the report above, labels can be dismissed from our lives altogether. They are temporary illusions, thoughts, and perceptions of the human conditioning. The truth is, the only power labels have is the power we choose to give them. As we step into more consciously evolving beings, the divine mind and divine heart will create a totally different picture. The good news is, you get to decide what that picture looks like.

The truth is . . . You are a free spirit. You have everything you need to help you soar. Listen to the voice within the silence. Your inner voice. Your inner knowing. Your inner truth. There is nothing you cannot overcome. There is no occasion that you cannot rise to. There is no mountain that is insurmountable. There is no depth that is too deep. You are not a particle within existence. You are the existence within a particle. The limiting beliefs that you have about yourself, are not from your internal world. They are simply external forces of resistance to build strength of spiritual character and the fortitude within you. You are not flawed, broken, limited, or deficient in anyway. No matter how much the external world pushes against your soul don't you dare believe it. Use that external resistance to build inner strength. Dare to defy the odds. Dare to defy all logic. Dare to defy indifference. Dare to defy limitation. Dare to defy those external voices that say to you you are not worthy, deserving, or enough. It is time to rise up past defeating doubts. It is time to claim our spiritual birth right, to be here, to be heard, to live as we were always intended to live; free, abundant, and holy. Its is time to release the shackles of fear, that have bound our hearts, and divided our souls as humans. It is time to expand our power and our divine connection to everything seen and unseen. To everything heard and unheard. To everything that encompasses who we are. We will no longer lay down with submissive apathy. We will rise up to a greater call which cannot and will not be ignored. We are temporarily human, yet we are eternally and magnificently divine. Claim your birth right. You are not the fear that the world so carelessly spreads. You are the force that dispels the fear. You are the light that can move through the night and bring us a new dawn of awakening. Let us stand together and answer the call to awaken the ascending human to a new level of one.

Mantra: *"I now release every limiting thought or belief I ever had about myself, for I AM a beautiful expression of love remembering the unfolding of my divine perfection."*

Chapter 62

Spiritual Manifesto
For Ascension

I now awaken to the divinity of the beautiful, intelligent light within me which is a pure expression of life in its fullness. I am on the perfect path of my awakened soul, which is now right before me, as I live a path of eternal truth. My spiritual and physical body are merging into compete oneness which is my spiritual birthright and has been from the beginning. I now activate the energy of my crown chakra, receiving divine light from heaven's gate flowing into my divine heart

I am now creating a life with harmonious creative intentions for the best and highest good of all beautiful souls seen and unseen. I embrace absolute truth that is stored within my inner knowing of the divine consciousness within, expanding daily within my consciousness. The light of universal consciousness is within me, connecting the elements of my mind, body and spirit with the divine mind of God. I now receive an inviting peace now resonating within all that I already am, the expanding peace within my heart.

I willingly explore the depths of my soul to know myself in its fullness, beyond the measures of time, distance and space, I see my life positively magnified and radiantly charged in all areas that encompass my being, mind, body and spirit. I now awaken the interdimensional aspects of my soul, moving through portals of conscious ascension and intention. I have access to eternal time through the portals of my soul, being free to explore the eternities of now . . . that I AM.

The hemispheres of my mind are now one, just as my mind and heart are now one, vibrating in the pure light of conscious love. I now rise and ascend with direct communication and communion with the angelic realms for healing and instruction. I claim my birthright by living the truth already within me, reconnecting to the I AM presence of God which is eternal and sure. I am always safe, protected and secure as the intervention of my heart knows how to discern my chosen path.

As I recognize I AM divine intelligence ascending, my spiritual and physical DNA become one pure intelligence even now. I am rooted and grounded within the pure womb of Mother Earth as the spirit of love nourishes my body, mind and soul. Conscious energy ignites passion within my divine awakening heart, empowering me to be the best version of me as I am now. I am at peace in my mind and heart and see myself as whole as I invite calmness into my entire being of brilliant illumination.

All memories within me are now restored in their fullness, expanding my views of life on every conceivable level. I now release and clear myself from feelings of bondage or any limiting patterns or behaviors, that no longer serve a purpose. I now call upon kundalini energy to move through my chakras, clearing, connecting and communicating the energies of divine light and love. I am balanced in the internal world of my mind and heart; therefore, I create balance energy in my earthly experiences.

I am now awakening Christ consciousness or the essence of universal love within my being for unity and oneness within all. I embrace the co-creative union between the divine masculine and divine feminine within me, which represents the wholeness of creation. Ancient wisdom and truth are always with me as I peer through the veil of my heart, trusting that I am remembering all aspects of my divinity.

I am now emerging through portals of my heart and into the birthing process of transformation and transfiguration. I trust in the incubation periods that my soul desires during this time, in preparation for new beginnings and enlightenment. I remember to nurture myself daily, as I awaken to the rising of the light within me, fostering peace, love, joy and acceptance for what is.

I envision the expansive expression of my experiences through the activation of my third eye now awakening to divine light and truth. The sum of my early and spiritual experiences and creations are equal to the expression of the joy I now feel in this moment of eternity now. I awaken to the origin of my soul and its purpose as I consciously choose the love that I am even now, as I remember the truth of love.

I now choose to see the true reflection of my soul as it moves through the portals of its divine purpose already unfolding as I reflect upon truth. I tune into the sacred sounds of spirit as I consciously listen to the true whisperings within my divine mind and heart. Vibrant light flows through me, grafting through me the pureness of spirit and all that encompasses the oneness of love eternal.

I am now connected to all that is revealed through the path of one, in all my relationships, past, present and future, including myself. I ascend as I live each day, connecting with the divine love of God and everything that emulates the peace and light in the path of love. I honor the divine masculine as a pillar of light, emulating a solid source of strength and truth to which I can rely upon right now. I honor the divine feminine now rising within me as a pillar of light, emulating the compassionate womb of love for which I can find rest.

I have clarity within the clear channels of my mind and heart, creating a solid bridge to the divine within. Vital energy flows through me in all areas of my abundant life, expanding more and more, as I live the truth of unconditional love. Everyday I rebirth the best version of myself as I remember to be open and teachable within my life experiences and creations. I am connected to both the heavens and the earth which support me both physically, mentally, emotionally and spiritually in abundance.

As I work through Karama, I now forgive all past deeds either remembered or not remembered releasing myself and others into the heart of forgiveness. My heart is sealed to universal love which is eternal intelligence through a divine creator to which I am infinitely a part of. I breathe life into the conceptions of my divine mind and heart, as I invite them to connect in creative ways. I now receive positive energy through every conscious breath which emulates and expands the life-giving breath of the I AM of God.

I now have clarity of thought as I awaken to the divine mind of God which is all encompassing in every divine expression of myself. I now unveil the truth within me, releasing any limiting or resisting energies that would keep me from knowing and seeing my light. I now send love to my ancestors who paved a path so that I might be as I am even now, which is their love living through me even now.

I now ground myself to the nurturing energies of Mother Earth and her ancient wisdom which connects me to the blessings of life. I am free to be a pure expression of love in its fullness through every aspect of my mind and heart as I am now creating their fullness. I am an infinite eternal being expressing and creating joy, love, peace and abundance for the unity of oneness and ascension. And so it is.

- Channeled by Leslie Paramore

Afterword

We all know truth, for the truth of divine spirit lives eternally within us. So when the ego mind is desperately driven to seek truth on the edge of the horizon of life, we will ultimately discover that the journey will lead us back to the source of all truth - the divine truth within. Truth is found when division no longer resides within us; when the ego mind is swallowed up in the illusion of life.

As we awaken to truth, we then invite the divine mind to become harmoniously ONE with the divine heart. It is then that the path of pure peace unfolds. In this moment of enlightened awakening, we no longer seek the destiny of heaven, for our very soul becomes heaven on earth. We become a beacon of pure love and light, accepting all, embracing all, loving all, becoming all. We then birth our soul to its greatest capacity, and in doing so, we ultimately become ONE with all that is and all that we are as conscious beings of light expanding.

~Leslie Paramore

Leslie Paramore operates a private practice, where she offers sessions globally and in person. She supports individuals on their path towards holistic health and wellness, mind, body, and spirit. She is a Heart Centered Reiki Master Teacher, Licensed Massage Therapist, Life Purpose Coach, Neuro Linguistic Practitioner, meditation recording artist, intuitive channeler and healer. She is passionate about supporting individuals in discovering their healing gifts and in supporting humanity toward global ascension. Along with her husband, Scott Paramore, she collaborates and creates playful videos to empower the minds and hearts of children.

To book a private session with Leslie, visit: *heartcenteredreiki.org*
To enroll in our online courses: *courses.heartcenteredreiki.org*
For children's empowerment: *sparklerprincess.com*

For more information on how you can help support our efforts please email: *info@heart-centered-productions.com*

Global Online Courses

Learn to tap into and harness universal life force energy to master the healing of your mind, body & spirit. Claim deep healing, clear energy blockages, melt into guided meditations and experience practical exercises that will leave you feeling lighter, stronger and freer. Get Certified as a Heart Centered Reiki Master Teacher.

Enroll here: https://courses.heartcenteredreiki.org/

*"**This course is amazing**, this is very very knowledgeable & user friendly course. I give 10 stars to this course!"*

\- Darshan

*"This course is positive & uplifting. **Leslie cares and is encouraging** to her students. Highly recommend this course."*

\- Rebecca

*"**This gave me so much hope** as I'm going through so much as I try to self heal. Thank you for giving me the opportunity!"*

\- Mya

If you are seeking greater balance for your life, integrate the tools offered in our Chakra Alignment Course for balancing, clearing, and restoring vital energy for each chakra. The 7 main energy wheels within our bodies, known as chakras, can be viewed through electromagnetic imaging. They work together along with our organ systems and help regulate balance, energy, vitality, and health. As an additional included bonus; 7 downloadable guided meditations for each chakra are included.

Enroll here: https://courses.heartcenteredreiki.org/

*This course is like a divine library, so much **information & wonderful** meditations. Thank you so much Leslie!*

-Amit

*Leslie is an amazing instructor! **The course if very comprehensive.** I've learned so much. Thank you for delivering instruction that will help so many people.*

- Cheryl

*Thank you for awakening my chakras through this course. It was **very nice and gratifying** to have done the meditations.*

-Vasco

Many energy healers worldwide are witnessing powerful results with their clients, by the use of our online course, "The 54 Angelic Symbols for Healing." These sacred symbols open energy fields within the body communicating healing frequencies, physically, emotionally, mentally, and spiritually. Expand your ability to channel deeper healing with Angelic Symbols for healing, as an energy practitioner or also, for personal use.

Enroll here: https://courses.heartcenteredreiki.org/

"Without a doubt, the most powerful and deeply effective healing modality I have ever taken. I have been trained in multiple modalities over the last 11 years and I'm so grateful (as are clients) to this beautiful healing process. I've seen miraculous transformations within myself and clients."

- Lisa

This course spoke to me like no other and I have enjoyed learning about the symbols. I have felt the energy of some of them, and can't wait to start using them in my practice. I love the way we never stop learning about the magic of the Universe.

-Theresa

Based on the content of this book, Leslie Paramore also offers, "The Art & Signs of Spiritual Awakening," in video format. Here she connects with you heart to heart. Designed to compliment her book and your life, you'll be invited to move into practical exercises that will support you in shifting from things that are no longer working for you in your life. Leslie gives specific assignments to move you closer to the awakened portions of you. *Note: The same material written within this book is presented in video format. Release in January 2022!

https://courses.heartcenteredreiki.org/

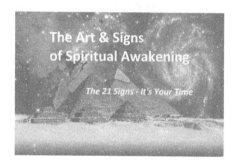

"It was through my own spiritual awakening process that I released this timely course for those who are struggling through the birthing pains of life. The video presentations will support you in reaffirming the concepts laid out within this book.

Life is a process of conscious decisions that will ultimately expand our experiences and perceptions of life. Consider enrolling in this course or gifting it to someone who is going through their own awakening. We appreciate your love and support and are grateful to have the opportunity to bless humanity in its ascension process."

-Leslie Paramore

Content for Children

We would be remiss if we neglected to highlight the work we are creating to empower the minds and hearts of children. Children everywhere deserve quality material that will teach them principles of kindness, courage, gratitude, curiosity, intelligence, politeness and other foundational tools that will support their own awakening process. Our has project has been an ongoing labor of love. Please take the time to visit our website: sparklerprincess.com to learn more about our vision for the children. We are looking for volunteers and financial contributors like you, to support a global mission that could quite literally change the world and the way we see our future generations. We have a vision for the children. We hope you can feel it too.

The Sparkler Princess & Bluey

Leslie Paramore is an international children's author with over 70 children's books written for the Korean educational system. Some of her titles have been produced into children's TV shows and cartoons in Korea. For the children globally, Leslie (The Sparkler Princess) offers her best work, "Anything's Possible. Anything Goes," a timeless book of empowerment for both children and adults. **Go to amazon.com and search: "The Sparkler Princess. Anything's Possible. Anything Goes."**

"This excellent book is light-hearted, cheerful and yet carries heartfelt messages reminiscent of Dr. Seuss' "Oh The Places You'll Go." Very uplifting for children of all ages!"

- Joanne Aber Ph.D.

Support Global Awakening for Humanity

It is our continued goal to bless humanity with material that supports the awareness, connection, and the healing of mind, body, and spirit. Thousands of hours of our hearts have been spent providing the best materials through manuals and high quality videos to provide empowering online courses. If you feel called to help expand our mission in supporting global healing, we so deeply appreciate any contributions for our cause.

With Much Love & Gratitude,
Leslie Paramore

PayPal Heart Centered Productions
https://www.paypal.com/paypalme/thesparklerprincess

Scan our QR code to donate.

Acknowledgments

Interior images by Pixabay.com
Many thanks to the artists at Pixabay for their beautiful artwork displayed within this book. I am so honored to share their art with you.

Cover image by:
Beate Bachmann https://pixabay.com/users/spirit111-5026413/

Content Contributors: Many thanks go to my friend, Leela Coccimigilo, for sharing her deeply moving story with the world. Her insights are invaluable. Additional thanks go to Owen Fitzgerald for sharing his personal eyewitness experience with the hurricane in Texas many years ago.

Student Testimonials: To my faithful students of my online courses, I appreciate your testimonials about your personal experiences with our health and wellness courses. Thank you.

Support: Deep gratitude is offered to my many friends, in person and global clients, family members, or anyone who has been a support and encourager in my life's journey. You know who you are and the Universe knows your name. Thank you. I extend further gratitude to individuals who are reading this book who choose to create change for their personal lives and for the betterment of humanity. I thank you for your support.

CPSIA information can be obtained
at www.ICGtesting.com
Printed in the USA
LVHW050256180122
708488LV00009B/214